CLIFF HOUSE HOTEL

THE COOKBOOK

WRITTEN BY **MARTIJN KAJUITER**

EDITED BY **TOM DOORLEY**

HOUGHTON MIFFLIN HARCOURT

Contents

Preface

I clearly recall the first time I tasted Martijn's food and experienced his cooking - I was blown away!

What a fantastic view! These are usually the first words uttered by visitors to The Cliff House Hotel as they walk into the lobby and stand at the glass balustrade whilst gazing over the expanse of Ardmore Bay in front of them.

There has of course been a hotel on this site since the early 1920's. We have only had the privilege of welcoming guests since opening the 'new' hotel in April 2008 but it has been very interesting to meet people who bring their elderly relatives to see the 'new' hotel having themselves been brought here as children during its past life.

Connecting the old and the new was very much part of the vision from the owners and this can be seen in the design itself and in the pictures of the old hotel dotted around the corridors. Indeed this connection has given the hotel an 'instant' soul that often takes a new hotel a long time to develop.

As a 'new' property, being involved from the beginning has allowed us to set a style and atmosphere for the hotel which I feel offers people who come and stay a very special experience and, at the same time, allows us to continue to be an integral part of the local community and surroundings. It is our wish to create a place where everyone is welcome and in which everyone will feel special.

Very soon after setting up the team who were going to run the hotel, I discussed the nature of the food we were going to serve with Martijn Kajuiter, the Head Chef. We spent many hours talking about what he had done in the past, what suppliers he had found in the area, the garden he had helped set up at St Raphael's in Youghal, what sort of food he was planning to offer and how he was going to prepare it.

Both Martijn and I could see the potential that could be achieved; a hotel that in addition to its stunning location, wide range of facilities, beautiful interiors and top-class bedrooms, could develop its own distinct personality with a service that would be personable and relaxed but professional at the same time.

Our dream is to provide a uniquely modern Irish hotel experience for our guests, one that will give The Cliff House Hotel its own strong and unique identity among Ireland's hospitality offerings. To this end we even have bespoke background music in the Bar, Restaurant and Spa – so that all five senses are addressed to give an overall experience of quality and attention to detail.

Having read the glowing reviews and received very positive feedback from our visitors to The Cliff House restaurant, we could see the potential to add a further dimension to the culinary experience of the hotel and quickly realised that it would be a good idea to compile a Cliff House Hotel Cookbook.

We had all the elements - a talented photographer in Andrew Bradley, a gifted chef in Martijn Kajuiter, and Ireland's top food journalist in Tom Doorley to bring it all together.

Little did we know how much work it would involve and how long it would take but we are extremely proud of the fruits of our labour and we hope that you will have as much enjoyment out of reading it as we did making it.

I look forward to welcoming you to The Cliff House Hotel so that you can see, feel, smell, taste and hear it for yourself.

Adriaan Bartels

General Manager - May 2009

Introduction

When somebody finally gets around to writing the history
of the Irish restaurant, it will be a slim volume.

There was a time - and it's not very long ago -
when we didn't really have restaurants in Ireland.

We had the grand hotels with their rigid formality,
varying stabs at classical French haute cuisine
and heavy sauces beneath which fresh produce,
local or otherwise, sank without trace.

When somebody finally gets around to writing
the history of the Irish restaurant, it will be a
slim volume. But you can be sure of one thing:
The Cliff House Hotel will loom large. And not
just because of its idyllic location and elegant,
modern design but because of the food.

Martijn Kajuiter is too modest to acknowledge it but he is undoubtedly a radical chef.
His approach to ingredients is very simple.

He goes right back to the drawing board and
asks himself what can be done with them,
avoiding all preconceived notions but occasionally giving a respectful nod to tradition,
where it is founded on common sense.

Very Dutch, really. But it's merely Dutch thinking.
His food is very, very Irish. This is, in part, due
to his utter devotion to local produce and his
respect for the culture in which he finds himself,
but I think he is actually paying Irish food the
highest compliment in that he is helping to
develop it.

I have worked closely with Martijn in getting
his recipes and his ideas on to the page, while
adding a few passages here and there off my
own bat. The result, I hope, is a clear picture of

where The Cliff House Hotel is, both physically
and culinarily.

In this sense, The Cliff House Hotel is in a very
special place - two very special places, indeed.
It's in Ardmore, one of the coastal jewels of all
Ireland and arguably the friendliest of them
all; and it's at the forefront of both showcasing
Irish food and gently but firmly pushing at
the boundaries.

But let me offer you a gentle warning, based on
personal experience. One visit is never enough.
There will be a part of every season when you
will wonder what Ardmore Bay looks like today
and what's on the menu at The Cliff.

Tom Doorley

Ardmore

Ardmore was a popular holiday destination for the
"big house" gentry of the county and from Cork.

We have Saint Declan to thank for the village of Ardmore. There are those who would argue to the contrary, but the local belief is that this native of the Decies was the first to bring Christianity to Ireland. However, St Patrick seems not only to have got the credit for this but to have been the dominant figure. Declan is said to have recognised Patrick's authority even though he was, along with his contemporaries Ailbhe, Ciaran and Ibar, a bishop before Patrick's arrival in Ireland in the fifth century AD.

Many Irish towns and villages owe their foundation to monasteries. Ardmore is a very ancient Christian site in that it was already established as a cathedral in 1170. St Declan's Oratory, situated near the church and round tower, is traditionally supposed to contain his burial place and is thought to date from the eighth century. An important ogham stone, probably from the time of Declan himself, was found within its walls in the last century.

The date of the round tower is uncertain but it seems likely to be a 12th century building. Nobody seems to know precisely why such towers were built and a great deal of doubt has been cast on the traditional notion that they were places of refuge into which monks could retreat, with the monastic treasures, during raids by the Vikings. They may have been simply bell towers. Whatever the original purpose, they are

a powerful symbol of Ireland (only a handful exist in Britain while they are well distributed here).

In time, Ardmore became a prosperous fishing village. Even today, it retains more fine houses than most such settlements and this reflects the fact that Ardmore was a popular holiday destination for the "big house" gentry of the county and from Cork. The gentry are virtually all long gone and Ardmore is no longer a fishing village: modern trawlers are too big, but a few small boats still go out in search of fish or to tend the lobster pots.

Ardmore has always had a strong attraction for writers. Molly Keane, the author of *Good Behaviour* and *Time After Time*, lived in the village and is buried in the Church of Ireland churchyard. The left-wing commentator Claud Cockburn was another resident and the American romantic novelist Nora Roberts has set three of her books in Ardmore. William Trevor, who grew up in Youghal, may have set some of his novel *The Story of Lucy Gault* at Ballyquin, right across the bay from The Cliff House Hotel.

Ardmore

Ardmore was a popular holiday destination for the landed gentry of East Munster.

Ardmore was a popular holiday destination for the landed gentry of East Munster. It attracted the Keanes, Musgraves, Jamesons, Perceval-Maxwells, Beresfords and Ansons to name just a few of the "big house" families who lived within thirty miles of Ardmore and who migrated there during the summer months.

The Odells of Carriglea, near Dungarvan, were minor gentry compared to the Musgraves and the Keanes who were titled, but they owned the land on which The Cliff House Hotel now stands. And, insofar as anyone can, they owned the beach below it.

It is thought that the original Cliff House Hotel was built as a holiday home for the Odells during the latter half of the nineteenth century. It was, of course, ideally suited to conversion into an hotel, given its position and its access to the beach. The gardens were terraced and there was a fine tennis court. Steep steps led down to a natural swimming pool below the hotel.

By the 1920s, The Cliff House, which was owned and run by the Kelly family, was the centre of an important part of Ardmore life. Molly Keane recalls how Joan Jameson, who lived in the village, and Norah McGuinness, two distinguished painters, would play serious card games there with their friends, the Nugents,

and other local enthusiasts: "Play might go on quite far into the night; even if Father Power had an early mass to celebrate, Paddy Spratt an important auction to conduct, or Joan a picture or a dead-line for some exhibition."

In 1936, the hotel was taken over by the founders' nephew, Frank Nugent, who lit the premises with a wind-powered generator in the days before rural electrification.

He remained in charge until his death in 1983 when the business passed to his son Aidan and his wife. The hotel was later sold to the Irwin family before being bought and redeveloped by the present owner.

The Decies

Everybody else in Ireland calls it County Waterford, but the people of these parts hold to an older tradition. In Waterford, the area is known as The Decies or, in Irish, An Deise. It seems that sometime between the fourth and fifth centuries AD a tribe of this name was driven from part of the south of Ireland and they settled in much of what is now the modern county of Waterford.

There has long been a tradition that the people of the Decies had been converted to Christianity long before the arrival of St Patrick, the man who is generally given credit for the conversion of Ireland. At this stage, it is impossible to say with certainty but in Co Waterford St Declan, the local man, tends to take precedence over the national saint.

The Decies has quite a wealth of prehistoric monuments, including some fine portal dolmens, which date from between 4000 and 3000BC, and stones bearing inscriptions in the ancient ogham alphabet which were probably created around the fourth century AD. There are many remains from the medieval period including the famous Reginald's Tower in Waterford City which was first built in 1003 but which, in its present form, is almost certainly a twelfth-century Norman building.

Geologically, the coastline of County Waterford is impressive, and reflects its volcanic origins. To the east of Ardmore lies the Copper Coast, named in recognition of the significance of copper mining to this area.

To the west, of course, is the town of Dungarvan which is the administrative capital of the county. And further to the west again is a most unusual feature of the area, the Gaeltacht of Ring or, in Irish, Rinn, near Helvick Head. The Irish language is still spoken on a daily basis here, never having died out. Such regions are very rare these days and tend to be found in the far west of Ireland.

Waterford, as somebody once wrote, is Ireland in a microcosm. You have a glorious coastline, undulating countryside, majestic rivers in the Suir and the Munster Blackwater, and rugged mountains: the Knockmealdowns and the Comeraghs to the north. Indeed, a visit to the mountain pass in the Knockmealdowns known as The Vee will allow you to see most of the county stretching away towards the sea, while behind you, is the vast flat expanse of Tipperary. Even in terms of agriculture, Waterford has a little of everything from lush dairy pastures and fertile cereal fields to hill farms of sheep and lambs.

So there you have it. The Decies or An Deise is, in effect, Ireland in miniature.

Umami and apples

This was my first umami moment. And that's something very important for someone who becomes a chef.

I was five, maybe six. It was a little restaurant at the local airport near Groningen that we used to go to on Sundays. My parents needed to get away from their snack bar. They were working with food all week, so there was no way they were going to cook Sunday lunch.

And in the winter, there was always oxtail soup on the menu: as brown as gravy, rich, intense, sticky. I remember sticking my finger in the bowl

of soup, when my mum and dad weren't looking, and sucking it.

This was my first umami moment. And that's something very important for someone who becomes a chef.

Umami is a Japanese word but it describes something that we all experience. It's the fifth taste. We all know sweet, sour, salty and bitter.

Umami is the taste, and sensation, that's missing from that traditional list.

How to describe it? I don't think anyone has come up with a really good definition yet. I'd say umami is a combination of rich savouriness and a kind of clinging silkiness. And that oxtail soup, all those years ago, had lots of it.

Like most kids, I was open to everything in the way of taste. I suppose I stuck my finger into that bowl of oxtail soup just to make sure I was going to like it and that's how I approached all food. And I was thorough. When I ate an apple, I chewed and swallowed the whole lot so that I got the whole taste.

When I picked wild berries, maybe I was dicing with death but it gave me a love of fruit, pure fruit and nothing but the fruit. Well, okay, I love the good old Dutch *haagse bluf* which is fruit purée folded into whipped egg whites: light and clean and really pure tasting.

I like to think that I'm still open to all tastes, all foods, but I know I'm not. I'll taste anything, eat anything but it won't always be with pleasure. I grew up in my parents' café and so I grew up with those awful hard-boiled eggs that have a grey ring all the way around the yolk. I have a phobia, a fetish, about eggs. Even today, I have to cook them myself.

Umami and apples

I don't get on too well with offal. I was brought up on pigs' liver, cooked until it was like leather. I would refuse to eat it at dinner and there it would be in the morning for breakfast. This was not a good start to my relationship with animal organs.

I was given a kidney dish recently in a restaurant that has two Michelin stars and even there it was an ordeal. I managed to get it down, and even though it was perfectly cooked and brilliantly thought out, it was like a punishment for me. Our tastes evolve, of course. Children hate bitter flavours but a lot of them grow up to like coffee and chicory, Angostura and even Guinness, all of which make bitterness part of their appeal. But I don't think I'll ever come to the stage where I say "You know, I'd really love some kidneys…"

But age is important. Restaurant cooking is for the young – or the fairly young – because it makes huge physical demands. Developing the sense of taste and the depth of experience to appreciate really fine restaurant cooking takes a lot of time so, in a sense, it's for older people or people who have packed a lot of living into a short time.

Anyway, maybe it was all those wild berries or the apples eaten whole but I developed a kind of mad idea – a really romantic idea – that real, proper cooking was about catching something or harvesting something and then dealing with it in the kitchen. Maybe I'm thinking backwards here but I do seem to remember that this was how I saw cooking when I was about thirteen or fourteen.

I had a rude awakening when I started in my first job, aged just fifteen, in a hotel kitchen. There was a huge stove with forty pork chops all at different stages of being cooked. It was mass production of food and it was then that I realised that restaurant food is different.

It was different in the great big hotel kitchen where I started my career and it's different here at The Cliff House. What's it different from?

It's different from home cooking, And it's different for one very important reason. When you or I cook at home, everything is done in one go. Okay, you can get a few things done ahead of time (some things even taste better when the flavours have had time to merge and intensify). But, overall, it's not like a restaurant kitchen where you have a team where everyone has a responsibility for various bits of the meal.

I had a rude awakening when I started in my first job,
aged just fifteen, in a hotel kitchen.

There's a flow to homecooking, a kind of harmony to the home kitchen that you just can't create in a restaurant.

There's a flow to homecooking, a kind of harmony to the home kitchen that you just can't create in a restaurant. Take just one very simple example. When you're cooking at home you can serve your meal with perfect new potatoes (one of the best things you can eat) that are just cooked. This just isn't possible in a commercial kitchen where time is such a critical factor.

By and large, restaurant kitchens don't foster creativity. Not because chefs are not interested in new dishes, new twists, new interpretations. It's just because the first question a chef asks about a dish, if he's being honest is "can I do this for 200 covers?"

I tend to laugh when I see risotto on a restaurant menu. Sure, you can produce something that's quite like a risotto with the stop-go cooking that a commercial kitchen demands. But it won't be a risotto. Not in my book. Because a proper risotto takes 25 minutes from the moment the rice hits the pan and you need one person to stir that pan, stopping only to add more stock. Practical? I don't think so. Risotto is so much better, so much truer when you make it at home, as I say, in one go.

So this book is about the food that we serve at The Cliff House Hotel. It's about the food that we source as close as possible to Ardmore and it's about what we do to it.

But it's a book for using at home. In that sense, you have an advantage over us because you can give each dish your undivided attention. And hopefully you won't be doing more than a dozen covers!

Soups

Potato soup with scallion

apple and almond

Ingredients

500g new potatoes, peeled

1 bunch scallions (spring onions)

4 free range eggs

1 Granny Smith apple, peeled and diced

100ml apple juice

600ml vegetable stock

olive oil / rapeseed oil

4 tsp almonds, crushed

garlic, bay leaf

3 peppercorns

seasoning

You can't ignore potatoes in Ireland. The good old spud is still quite central to how people eat and it is very much the Irish version of starch, taking the place that bread, rice or pasta occupies in other cuisines.

At The Cliff House we like to acknowledge the centrality of the potato but we try to do it with a light touch and sometimes with a sense of humour. You won't get a big dollop of mash with your dinner here but the potato will crop up during the meal, sometimes in unusual forms and occasionally unexpectedly.

This soup involves only Irish ingredients and the colours are those of the Irish flag, the Tricolour.

- Cut one of the potatoes into large cubes.

- Place them in a pot and cover them with rapeseed oil.

- Add ½ clove of garlic, 3 crushed peppercorns and a bay leaf.

- Simmer the potato until cooked through.

- The remaining potatoes will go to make the soup.

- Bring the vegetable stock to a quick boil and add the remaining potatoes.

- Cook them until tender.

- Slice the scallions, putting two of them aside for the garnish.

- Strain the potatoes and reserve the cooking stock.

- Mash the potatoes and add 2 tbsp of olive oil.

- Put the cooking stock in a blender and add the scallions.

- Blend until smooth; add 1 tbsp of olive oil and the apple juice.

- Then mix with the mash and return to the saucepan.

- Check the consistency. If it is too thick, just add some more stock.

- Bring to the boil and season to taste.

- Warm 4 large deep plates.

- Warm the potato cubes with the apple and add the scallions.

- Separate the eggs and place the egg yolk in the middle of the plates.

- Divide the potato, apple and scallion mix over the 4 plates and add the almonds.

- Gently pour in the soup and serve.

Soup of cottiers' kale

with crouton and grilled rasher

Ingredients

500g cottiers' kale

750ml vegetable stock

250g Golden Wonder potatoes
peeled, washed and cut into quarters

125ml cream

butter

1 clove garlic

olive oil, salt, pepper

2 white bread rolls

3 streaky rashers per person

You could almost be forgiven for thinking that cottiers' kale is a myth. You can't buy seeds and the only way to get some for your garden is to find someone who has some and root some cuttings.

I first read about cottiers' kale in an old Irish cookery book and I was determined to find this particular edible plant. When I googled it, the only hit referred to one of the Ballymaloe cookbooks, so I wrote to Darina Allen. She very kindly invited me over – it's only half an hour from here – to get some cuttings. I can confirm that it roots very easily and it seems to go on forever (but I'm told it's best to take new cuttings every three years in order to keep it leafy).

Cottiers' kale looks more like a cabbage than a true kale but it has a really intense flavour and, best of all, it contains virtually no fibres or stalks or tough bits. It's one of my treasured possessions in the garden.

It took only two months to get a fine, leafy harvest and we started working with it on the menu at The Cliff House. We sliced it very finely and served it raw as a salad, made soup from it, and incorporated it into a nice mash. Here it makes an unusual soup.

- Pre-heat the oven to 170°C.

- Put aside a few nice leaves for the garnish. Take a large pot, pour in the vegetable stock and bring to the boil.

- Add the kale leaves and cook them for 1 minute. Drain. Purée the cooked kale in blender with 2 tbsp of olive oil and season to taste.

- Now add the potatoes, garlic and cream to the stock and simmer this until the potatoes are tender.

- Break the bread rolls into small chunks, drizzle with olive oil and season with salt. Bake until golden brown and crisp in the oven.

- Blend the soup in a food processor until smooth. Return to the pot and bring to the boil; add the kale purée and season.

- Grill the rashers on both sides until crisp.

- Melt some butter and toss the reserved leaves in it.

- Pour the soup into bowls and arrange the bread croutons on top.

- Arrange the rashers and kale leaves in the soup and drizzle over the remaining butter. Grind some black pepper over all and serve.

Parsnip soup with marsh samphire

broad beans and lemon

Ingredients

750g parsnips, peeled

oil

salt and pepper

1 onion, chopped

1 leek, sliced

1 potato, diced

750ml vegetable stock

250ml cream

Garnish

60g broad beans

50g marsh samphire

rind of a lemon, cut in thick strips

In a lot of restaurants you ask what is the soup of the day and the answer will always be the same. Vegetable. And why? Because the soup of the day is an exercise in economy, using up leftovers and trimmings. Most of the time what arrives at your table is pure waste, in every sense of the word.

Well, this is one reason why we take soup seriously at The Cliff House. Our soups focus on one or maybe two key ingredients and they have to be really good. We are very particular about this.

The humble parsnip is a vegetable that makes an exceptional soup. It has a fresh, earthy, sweet flavour that is generally very under-appreciated, probably because parsnips are cheap and plentiful. Parsnip soup is one dish that really can brighten up your day - if it's properly made.

Serve it with some warm, buttered soda bread.

- Pre-heat the oven to 175°C.

- Take two parsnips and put aside.

- Place the remaining parsnips on an oven tray and sprinkle with oil, salt and pepper.

- Roast for about 15 minutes.

- Put the leek, onion, potato and roast parsnips into a large pot and cover with the stock.

- Bring to the boil, then simmer until all the vegetables are soft.

- Purée to a smooth soup using a hand-blender.

- Bring to the boil and season to taste.

- Bring a pot of salted water to the boil.

- Peel the remaining parsnips and with the peeler turn them into long strips.

- Drop the parsnip strips into the boiling water and when it returns to the boil, add the broad beans.

- After 2 minutes strain and add the samphire, a tablespoon of olive oil and the strips of lemon rind.

- Toss and season.

- Whip the cream and fold into the soup.

- Arrange the garnish in the centre of the soup bowls and pour the soup around it.

Colcannon soup

with boiled bacon and mustard

Ingredients

250g Golden Wonder potatoes,
peeled and quartered

100g white onions, sliced

100ml cream

250g milk

500ml vegetable stock

70g butter

400g cottier's kale or curly kale leaves
(cabbage will do) without stalks

50ml rapeseed oil

4 slices of boiled streaky bacon

English mustard

Colcannon is one of Ireland's great potato dishes. In Holland we have something similar called stampot boerenkool. It contains the same ingredients but is served with big smoky sausage and thickly sliced boiled bacon, a great winter dish.

Colcannon somehow became the theme of the first amuse bouche at The Cliff House. Essentially, we deconstructed the colcannon by preparing all ingredients separately in different ways and then assembling them all in a martini glass.

The potatoes were boiled and smoked and turned into a fluffy mash; the kale was sliced into fine filaments to create a raw salad; onions were braised with thyme; and from the water in which the potatoes had been cooked, we made parsley "air cloud" to finish it.

But don't worry! That's not what we're going to do here. We'll just look at what we believe colcannon should, in essence, be, but in the form of a soup rather than a vegetable dish.

By the way, there is an old Irish tradition of hiding coins in the colcannon for the children to find as they tuck into their Halloween dinner, the time when colcannon is traditionally served.

Traditionally, it goes with boiled bacon, but you can try it with some belly pork and a good scoop of mustard.

- Cook the potatoes and onions in the vegetable stock with the cream, milk and butter.

- Blanch the kale in boiling salted water until tender.

- Put the hot leaves in a blender and add a cup of the boiling water and the oil.

- Blend to a smooth purée.

- When the potatoes and the onions are cooked use a hand blender to create a smooth soup.

- Now add the kale purée and season to taste.

- Place 2 pieces of bacon in each soup bowl.

- Strain and pour into soup bowls.

- Place a generous dab of mustard on each piece of bacon.

The Cliff House seafood chowder

Ingredients

250g onion, diced

500g potato, peeled and diced

1 ltr fish stock

500g mixed seafood (e.g. cod, salmon, monkfish, prawn, mussels, clams)

1 large potato, peeled and cut into chunks

2 tbsp chopped parsley

100ml cream

zest of 1 lemon

People are choosy about chowder. It can mean different things to different people. One person's ideal version is loaded with cream, another's is about delicate seafood flavours and light texture. The problem is, of course, that in a restaurant you have to take positions on things like this.

At The Cliff House, we start off with a definition that goes like this:

Chowder is a soup made on a base of fish or shellfish stock with onion, potato and a rich addition of several chunks of fish, shellfish and crustaceans, finished with fresh parsley, lemon and a dash of cream.

That's the guideline that we use but do remember that's all it is.

- Put onion, potato and fish stock into a pot.
- Bring to a soft boil and cook until the potatoes are soft.
- Blend this mixture to a fine soup.
- Add the potato chunks and simmer for 8 minutes.
- Season to taste and add the mixed fish.
- Then simmer for another 5 minutes.
- Add the cream, lemon zest and chopped parsley.
- Check seasoning and serve.

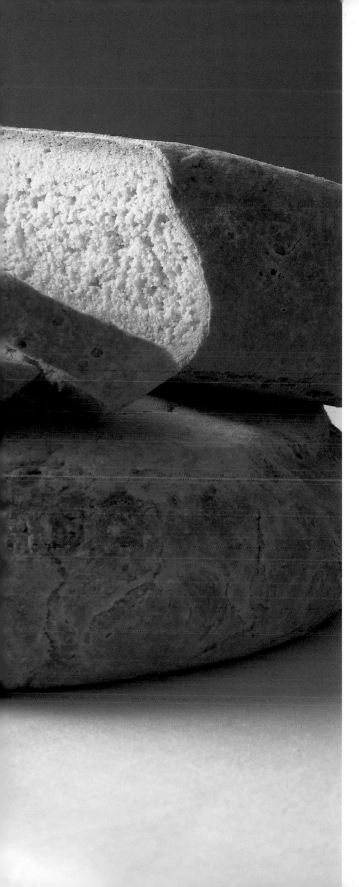

Breads

Granny McGrath's brown soda bread

Ingredients

700g coarse wholemeal flour

300g fine wholemeal flour

200g wheatgerm

200g porridge oats

200g brown sugar

200g bran

½ tbsp salt

3 eggs, beaten

1.5 ltr buttermilk

1½ tbsp bread soda

Brown soda bread is one of Ireland's great contributions to the world of food. It is unique and more Irish than stout and peat fires. At The Cliff House, brown soda bread is a staple, baked freshly every morning.

Like all classics, there are as many recipes as there are people who bake it and usually they are handed down from generation to generation. It's the same with us. Our recipe comes by way of Shane McGrath, my sous-chef. His grandmother cooked it all her life and, as usual with old family recipes, she never actually weighed anything. It was all calculated by the eye, and made entirely by hand.

Shane very sensibly got her to cook him a loaf one day and as soon as she had assembled all the ingredients he made the measurements and wrote it all down. So Shane has preserved an important piece of family heritage and given us what I think is the best recipe for soda bread.

In the days before pasteurisation, milk could turn sour after a few days without going nasty. This is what Shane's grandmother originally used but nowadays buttermilk is the answer. It, too, has plenty of lactic acid which reacts with the baking soda to form little bubbles of carbon dioxide. This is what makes the bread rise.

You will need two big loaf tins.

- Pre-heat the oven to 170°C.

- Put all the dry ingredients into a large mixing bowl.

- Add the buttermilk and the eggs.

- Mix all together until a fluffy texture is achieved.

- Grease the baking tins with butter and divide the bread mix between them.

- Bake for 60 minutes.

- Remove the bread from the tins.

- Turn the loaves and replace them in the tins.

- Bake for a further 10 minutes.

- Remove from the tins and let cool on a wire rack.

Sea vegetable brioche

Ingredients

For 4 small loaves

500g flour

25g yeast

10g salt

5g sugar

100g melted butter or olive oil

175ml warm milk

125ml eggs, beaten

50g dried chopped sea vegetables

2 egg yolks with a dash of milk
for the egg wash glaze

Maldon sea salt flakes

There is a saying: serve good bread and all will be well. At The Cliff House, we agree. And we make our own bread because it's an opportunity to give guests something unique to us.

Dinner here always starts with a slice of Glenilen farmhouse butter from West Cork and a small loaf of homemade brioche flavoured with sea vegetables. We make only one bread to accompany the dinner instead of six mediocre ones. We like the sea theme; it's very appropriate for where we are.

Why brioche? Well, it's the combination of light texture and crisp crust.

- Pre-heat the oven to 190°C.

- Mix the milk and the eggs.

- Mix in the yeast and the dried sea vegetables with a hand blender.

- Sieve the flour and add the sugar and salt.

- Make dough with the milk/egg mixture and the flour, adding the melted butter slowly to it.

- Work the dough for about 5 minutes on a well-floured work surface.

- Divide into 4 pieces and make 4 tight dough balls of it.

- Put on baking tray, and brush the dough with the egg wash.

- Then sprinkle with sea salt flakes.

- Let the dough rise in a warm place for about an hour.

- Bake for 20 minutes.

- Check if the bread is cooked by sticking a skewer in it. If it comes out clean, it's done.

- Leave to cool and serve.

Red currant bread

Ingredients

600g organic flour

330ml warm water

80ml rapeseed oil

12g salt

25g yeast

1 tbsp chopped thyme

250g red currants

coarse sea salt

honey

When you're planning a picnic, it's good to get away from sliced pan and shop bread. This is a lovely alternative, very versatile and quick to make.

The base is focaccia dough that I discovered during one of my culinary trips to Italy. Essentially, it's a flat bread that you can dress with whatever comes to hand. Grapes, surprising as it may seem, work very well but cherry tomatoes and other red fruits have just the right colour and acidity.

And so, for this Irish version of focaccia, we use fresh red currants with thyme, honey and sea salt. It's great with cured ham and salad or perhaps smoked salmon with a little cream cheese.

- Pre-heat the oven to 200°C.

- Mix the flour, salt and thyme in a bowl.

- Mix the yeast with the water and add the oil.

- Add to the flour mixture and work it through until a firm dough is produced.

- Let the dough rest for 15 minutes.

- Flour the work surface and roll the dough out to fit a baking tray.

- Slide the dough on to the baking tray.

- Sprinkle on the currants and lightly press into the dough.

- Drizzle with honey and sprinkle with sea salt.

- Let the dough rise for 20 minutes in a warm place.

- Bake the bread for at least 20 minutes.

- Check if the bread is cooked using a skewer. If it comes out clean, the bread is done.

- Remove from the oven and let it cool.

- Cut in rectangular pieces.

Basic white bread rolls

Ingredients

For brown bread, replace the white flour with fine wholemeal

500g plain white flour

15g yeast

10g salt

300ml warm water

40g soft butter

- Pre-heat the oven to 200°C.

- Sieve the flour.

- Make a hollow in the centre.

- Pour the water into the hollow and crumble in the yeast.

- Mix the flour gently with the water and yeast, using your fingers.

- Knead the dough for 5 minutes on a floured work surface and shape into a ball.

- Cover with a tea towel, put in a warm place, and let it rise for 45 minutes.

- Then knock back the dough (in other words deflate it by kneading) and work the butter and salt through it.

- Divide into 20 small pieces and shape into balls.

- Put on a baking tray.

- Brush with a little water.

- Let rise for another 45 minutes.

- Then bake for 18 minutes.

- Check if the bread is cooked (if a skewer comes out clean, it is) and let it cool on a rack.

Parsley bread

- Pre-heat the oven to 200°C.

- Blend milk with the parsley until smooth and green.

- Dissolve the yeast in this mixture.

- Sieve the flour and add the salt.

- Make a hollow in the centre of the flour and pour in the parsley and milk mixture.

- Mix the flour gently with the yeast and the milk, using your fingers.

- Knead the dough for 5 minutes on a floured work surface and shape into a ball.

- Cover with a tea towel, put in a warm place, and let it rise for 45 minutes.

- Then knock back the dough (in other words deflate it by kneading) and work the butter through it.

- Make into a ball and then roll it in a cylinder shape.

- Put on a baking tray.

- Brush with a little water.

- Let rise for another 45 minutes.

- Bake for 20 minutes. If a skewer comes out clean, it's cooked.

- Cool on a wire rack.

Ingredients

500g plain white flour

25g yeast

240ml warm milk

10g salt

1 bunch parsley

butter

Irish spelt bread with Beamish

honey and thyme

Ingredients

500g spelt flour

350ml Beamish stout

20g yeast

20g salt

20g honey

¼ bunch of thyme

honey

sea salt flakes

- Pre-heat the oven to 200°C.
- Make a hollow in the centre of the flour.
- Mix the honey and crumbled yeast with the Beamish and pour into the hollow.
- Gradually mix with the flour using your fingers.
- Knead the dough for 10 minutes and shape into a ball.
- Cover with a tea towel and let it rise for 45 minutes.
- Knock back the dough and add the salt.
- Knead the dough again and shape into a loaf.
- Brush with a little water.
- Cut shallow diagonal stripes in the top.
- Strip the leaves from the thyme.
- Sprinkle with honey, thyme and sea salt.
- Let it rise for another 45 minutes.
- Bake for 35 minutes.
- Check if the bread is cooked through and let it cool on a rack.

Pan-fried white soda bread

Ingredients

500g plain flour

50g sugar

15g salt

1 tsp bread soda

500ml buttermilk

It may seem a bit strange to cook bread in a frying pan but this approach produces a superb loaf. It was inspired, in many ways, by the traditional way of cooking soda bread in Ireland, in the days before ovens were commonplace in the countryside.

- Pre-heat the oven to 160°C.

- Sieve the flour, bread soda, sugar and salt into a mixing bowl.

- Make a well in the middle and pour in the buttermilk.

- Mix with a wooden spoon until all is combined.

- Then put out on to a floured work surface and knead until you have a smooth dough.

- Shape into a round, 3cm thick.

- Heat a non-stick frying pan with a knob of butter and a little flour.

- Place the bread dough in the pan and cook gently for 15 minutes on each side.

- Finish the bread by putting it in the oven for 10 minutes.

Butters

In Holland we say that butter is gold. And here in Ireland people think the same way. Butter is precious stuff and the Irish can't get enough of it.

At The Cliff House we use proper, old-fashioned farmhouse butter from the Kingston family at Glenilen in West Cork. This butter is so good that it reminds me of home and it really is a flavour bomb. It gives you the true taste of the land from where it comes.

Of course, most people are just not used to real butter like this. A lot of our guests don't like Glenilen and some even think that it has gone off! This is what butter is meant to taste like. It's just that the Dairy Mafia of Ireland has washed all the true taste out of the big brand butters.

Butter is amazingly versatile. It is used in many ways but has a special role in sauces and pastry. And, of course, with good bread it is your best friend.

One thing that most people don't realise about butter is the way it can absorb and carry other flavours so well. Here are just a few ideas for marrying lovely tastes with lovely butter.

- All of these recipes are based on a base of 250g salted butter.
- Make sure that the butter is at room temperature (you can soften it in the microwave if need be).
- If you want a softer butter, just blend in a tablespoon of olive oil.

These flavoured butters go beautifully with just about anything savoury. With fish, meat, poultry, just pick a flavour to partner it and have a go. Here are some ideas...

Butter with roasted garlic and parsley
50g roasted garlic purée (see page 56)
½ bunch flatleaf parsley, chopped
½ lemon, zest and juice

Butter with honey and mustard
75g Dijon mustard
40ml local organic honey

Butter with horseradish and lemon
80g grated horseradish
2 lemons, zest and juice

Butter "tartare"
1 tbsp chopped shallot
1 tbsp chopped capers
1 tbsp chopped pickled gherkins (cornichons)
2 tbsp chopped chervil
1 tbsp chopped tarragon
1 tsp chopped garlic

Butter with Cashel Blue
100g Cashel Blue cheese (at room temperature and mashed with a fork)

Butter with bay leaf
100g fresh bay leaves (briefly blanched in boiling water and blended into a purée)

Making the flavoured butters:

- Combine the butter with the other ingredients in a large mixing bowl.

- Season the mixture with pepper and put it in a piping bag with a wide nozzle.

- Spread a double layer of clingfilm on the work surface and pipe the butter mixture onto it.

- Roll up in the shape of a sausage and close the ends.

- Put in the fridge for at least 1 hour and then slice in rounds.

The garden

We Irish are not great vegetable eaters, despite our historic and continuing obsession with the potato. In a sense, it is quite significant that the chef at The Cliff House is not an Irishman, because here the menu celebrates rather than tolerates the produce of the kitchen garden.

Even these days, when Irish supermarkets sell scallions from Mexico and asparagus from Peru, the coastal farming land of West Waterford and East Cork is still known for fine carrots and potatoes and, thanks to the relatively mild climate, for early crops. And small producers still survive, not all of them organic but working on sound old principles. In butchers' shops in these parts you will see their produce, usually encrusted with a bit of sandy soil, something that underlines the fact that they were both sown and harvested by hand. No plastic flow-wrap for them! And no supermarket consistency of size or shape.

And so there is a sense of connection with the land and a degree of pride in eating local produce, something that has been largely lost in the towns and cities.

But the kind of menus that Martijn Kajuiter creates at The Cliff House Hotel pushes at the boundaries of the average person's experience of vegetables in Ireland. We are passionate about potatoes, as I say, and quite keen on cabbage,

sprouts and swedes. Restaurants extend the selection to broccoli and carrots even creating an unintentional representation of the national flag, the tricolour. Such things don't bring any cheer. They are merely tokens, a nod to the concept of the five-a-day.

Martijn's menus look way beyond such staples. He is, as he says himself, a chef and not a gardener, but he talks with a gardener's enthusiasm and sense of seasonality. Seasonality is something that has been all but lost thanks to air miles. Strawberries are no longer a treat in June if you can buy them in December.

And seasonality imposes its own pattern and discipline on menus. Especially in the notorious "hungry gap" that stretches over much of April and May, when fresh produce is at its scarcest and the new crops are yet to ripen.

The Cliff House benefits from exceptionally fresh and local produce with all the extra flavour and texture that this involves. But thanks to Martijn's enthusiasm, there is a further taste bonus in the form of the so-called heritage or heirloom vegetable varieties that feature frequently on his menus.

These are, essentially, varieties that have almost died out, ones that were once commercially

useful but which have been superseded by bigger, glossier versions with longer shelf life. And, usually, with less flavour and character.

The one vegetable - or fruit, to be precise about it - that has suffered most from this dilution of flavour is the tomato and, thankfully, there is now huge demand for tomatoes that would have been familiar to our great-grandparents. The availability of seed of such varieties means that heritage tomatoes are a key part of summer at The Cliff House.

A lot of people think that salad is salad, green stuff that is good for you. This is thanks to the fact that the world is dominated by a handful of commercial varieties which have been bred for their ability to look fresh longer and with little or no reference to flavour or, indeed, texture. But the range of varieties available to the home grower or to market gardeners who are prepared to work a little bit harder and seek the right kind of buyers, is vast. Not only are there lettuces, batavians, endives, rocket, purslane and mache but also a whole world of oriental salad plants, many of them with the peppery bite of the cress family. Again, this diversity is actively celebrated at The Cliff House throughout the culinary year.

Martijn Kajuiter is the kind of chef who makes daily visits to the garden in order to see what is

The Cliff House benefits from exceptionally fresh and local produce with all the extra flavour and texture that this involves.

The emphasis on fresh local produce may have seemed, ironically, a little exotic when the hotel opened but by now such notions are going mainstream.

ready and to plan what to do with it. Much of the kitchen's vegetable needs are supplied by St Raphael's in nearby Youghal, a residential and day-care centre for 150 people with intellectual disabilities.

Part of the therapeutic programme here is a garden with polytunnels which initially concentrated on growing lettuce for the local market. Now they grow to order for The Cliff House and are happy to try experimental crops All of the hotel's chefs are encouraged to visit regularly, to taste and watch what is coming close to ripeness or harvesting and to pick only what is needed so as to avoid waste.

Of course, there is no consistency of supply, which is what the average restaurant kitchen demands. For that you need commercial growers in the different parts of the world, but The Cliff House Hotel gets consistency of commitment, which is much more important. And the people who are involved in the work of growing come close to the miracle of plant life and share in the wonder of it. It provides an outlet for people whose powers of actual verbal expression are often very limited but who, as Martijn says, don't want to be pampered or patronised. They do very important work and they can take credit for a great deal of good food.

Liam Kelly, a retired teacher who lives near Youghal, grows vegetables to order for the hotel kitchen and not only provides the likes of herbs and kale but also exotics like seakale and marsh samphire. And knowing where to find marsh samphire is a rare and wonderful skill which would be treasured by many chefs.

The emphasis on fresh local produce may have seemed, ironically, a little exotic when the hotel opened but by now such notions are going mainstream. Allotments are in demand, seed potatoes sell out in jig time, and lawns are being dug up these days. There is a new awareness in the air, spades are being wielded once again.

Can it be that our national reservations about the vegetable kingdom are being eroded at last? If so, much of the credit must go to restaurants like that at The Cliff House Hotel where they get the respect that they deserve. And that's what good cooking is all about. It's about respect, pure and simple.

Vinaigrettes

At The Cliff House we take dressings very seriously but we like to play with them a bit. Of course, we make our own flavoured and infused oils and vinegars so as to get a whole range of flavours to experiment with.

Most people tend to think of a vinaigrette only as something that you have with salad. True, a really good dressing is something that makes a good salad into a great salad. But there is more to the vinaigrette than that. There is hardly a single savoury dish, and few sweet dishes, that won't be enlivened by one.

At The Cliff House we take dressings very seriously but we like to play with them a bit. Of course, we make our own flavoured and infused oils and vinegars so as to get a whole range of flavours to experiment with.

Even the rind of a lemon or some crushed garlic will give oil an immediate and direct hit of extra flavour but if you are using, say, rosemary or vanilla it will take longer. It is much the same with vinegars but the acidity level is so high that some flavours can be obliterated in a very short time. For example, basil is a very fragrant and aromatic herb and it infuses brilliantly in oil. Try it in vinegar and the aroma and flavour vanish completely in only a couple of hours.

Most people never think about it, but water has an important role in vinaigrettes. It builds a kind of bridge for flavours as it surrounds the oil molecules. Acidity, in the form of lemon, vinegar or mustard, helps this emulsification process while the water provides a vehicle for taste and sometimes even colour.

We use five basic types of vinaigrette in our kitchen at The Cliff House and this is how they break down:

- The basic salad vinaigrette
- The split vinaigrette
- The emulsified vinaigrette
- The warm vinaigrette
- The sweet vinaigrette

One word of advice. While whatever vinaigrette you make is up to you, it's essential to respect the vital balance between oil and acid. Once you do that, you can play around with all the ingredients to your heart's conent.

The basic vinaigrette

This is the first thing chefs learn in catering school. It's always good with salad or for marinating tomatoes and cucumbers. And if you experiment with it you can use it with strawberries (just remember to replace the groundnut oil with olive oil, the vinegar with balsamic, the parsley with tarragon and the shallot with apple). The French also make a less fatty version by replacing one part oil with water.

3 tbsp groundnut oil
1 tbsp vinegar
½ tbsp chopped shallot
½ tbsp chopped parsley
pepper and salt for seasoning

- Pour the vinegar into a mixing bowl and season it with a small pinch of salt and pepper.
- Add the oil spoon by spoon and stir well.
- Add the shallot and parsley.
- Save the vinaigrette in a small container for use later.

The split vinaigrette

The split vinaigrette is one that holds a component of flavour that "floats" in the oil and vinegar mixture. The effect can go beyond just flavour in that it can sometimes create a colour palette on the plate too.

We return to the less fatty version of the basic vinaigrette and instead of adding water we use carrot juice that has been reduced to a thick consistency and replace the vinegar with lemon juice. But because lemon is more tart than vinegar we use only half a tablespoon.

Vinaigrette of hazelnut and carrot

2 tbsp hazelnut oil
1 tbsp carrot juice
(Take 100ml of carrot juice and add ⅙ leaf of gelatine; simmer on a low heat until the amount is reduced to a tablespoon)
½ tbsp lemon juice
1 tbsp roasted and crushed hazelnuts
seasoning

Mix all ingredients together and serve. This vinaigrette is particularly good with roasted fish or a salad of vegetables.

The emulsified vinaigrette

This is our house vinaigrette, the one that we use to dress most of our salads. But why do we use an emulsified vinaigrette? The reason is very simple: it clings more effectively to the surface of the salad leaves and by doing that it delivers the extra flavour and punch that we want. We always make a whole bottle, hence the large amounts!

300ml groundnut oil
100ml olive oil
200ml organic apple juice
2 tbsp mustard
juice and zest of a lemon
salt

- Put the lemon juice, lemon zest, mustard and salt in a mixing bowl.
- Gradually whisk in the oils, in a thin stream, until everything is combined and you have a thin mayonnaise.
- Add the apple juice and season.
- Pour into a bottle and store until use in the fridge.

A sweet vinaigrette may seem a bit unusual but this one is
served with desserts where the richness needs to be cut.

The warm vinaigrette

Because this kind of vinaigrette contains aromatic herbs and small pieces of vegetables, it doesn't keep. Don't try to warm it up again! You only have one chance with it because over quite a short time the vinegar loses the flavours with which it has been infused and the vegetable elements lose their freshness and go rather dull.

In winter time I make warm vinaigrette with lentils and it suits the season. But in summertime warm fennel vinaigrette can be great with fish and shellfish dishes, especially barbecued mackerel. It is also good with grilled beef and poultry.

Warm tomato, fennel and white bean vinaigrette

250ml olive oil
70ml white wine vinegar
1 cubed plum tomato
½ cubed fennel bulb
50g white beans, cooked
1 tbsp shallot, chopped
1 tbsp fennel leaves, chopped
1 tbsp chives, finely sliced
½ tbsp tarragon, chopped
zest of 1 lemon
seasoning

- Warm the oil and add the fennel and beans; keep on a low heat for 5 minutes.
- Add the tomato, shallot and lemon zest, and mix.
- Season and add the herbs.
- Stir in the vinegar.
- Check the seasoning and serve directly.

The sweet vinaigrette

A sweet vinaigrette may seem a bit unusual but this one is served with desserts where the richness needs to be cut. Think of caramelised apple or chocolate fudge. Both are overwhelmingly sweet and bursting with flavour, but in my opinion they need something sharp. That sharpness will enhance the explosion of flavour and your ability to taste. It is not too powerful and works simply as an enhancement.

Irish coffee vinaigrette

3 tbsp olive oil
½ tbsp orange juice
1 tbsp espresso coffee
½ tbsp Irish whiskey
1 tsp cocoa powder
1 tsp brown sugar
salt and cream

- Combine the sugar and the cocoa powder in a mixing bowl with the coffee, orange juice and whiskey.
- Make sure that the ingredients dissolve fully and add a pinch of salt.
- Drop by drop, whisk in the olive oil.
- Serve with vanilla ice cream, chocolate mousse or warm fruits. Spoon the vinaigrette onto the plate, then put a few drops of cream on top to complete the Irish Coffee effect.

Vegetables

Vegetables

Vegetables are very important at The Cliff House and the following recipes will give you some idea of how we like to use them, not as the usual afterthought but with the respect that they deserve.

Roasted garlic

This is very simple and it will give you tons of flavour. We cook the garlic in their skins. What happens is that the sugars in the garlic start to caramelise and release a flavour intensity that is absolutely fabulous. You can make a big batch in advance and store the purée in a jar in the fridge for at least a week, but do watch it carefully. If you don't cover it securely the whole fridge will be tainted. We add roasted garlic to sauces and to butters in order to give them more depth.

6 whole garlic bulbs
rapeseed oil

- Put the garlic on an oven tray.
- Roast at 150°C for 50 minutes.
- When cool, cut off the top of the garlic and squeeze out the soft flesh.
- Push through a sieve and add a dash of oil.
- Mix the purée well.
- Store in a jar in the fridge.

Oven-roasted brussels sprouts

500g fresh sprouts, cleaned
1 shallot
1 clove garlic
150ml aged malt vinegar
pepper, salt, butter, rapeseed oil.

- Pre-heat the oven to 170°C.
- Blend the shallot, garlic and vinegar in a food processor for 1 minute.
- In a heated pan fry the sprouts in a little oil until they start to colour.
- Pour the vinegar mixture on the sprouts and bring to the boil.
- Transfer to an oven dish and cover with tin foil.
- After 30 minutes remove the foil and cook the sprouts further until very tender and until most of the vinegar has evaporated - which will take about another 30 minutes.
- Then add a knob of butter and season to taste.

Carrot purée with orange and cardamom

The trick here is to cook the carrots with the minimum amount of liquid. We use a vacuum bag but at home a pressure cooker will do just as well.

500g carrots, peeled and diced into 1cm cubes
1 orange
1 tsp cardamom
pepper, salt, butter
½ leaf of gelatine
1tbsp olive oil

- Put a tablespoon of butter in a pressure cooker and add the cardamom seeds. Put it on low heat, uncovered.
- Peel the zest of the orange and add to the butter. Peel the pith from the orange, dice up the flesh and add to the butter.
- Now add the carrots and ½ cup of vegetable stock or water.
- Put the lid on and turn up the heat.
- Boil for 20 minutes. Strain the carrots but save the liquid.
- Put the carrots in a blender and add seasoning.
- Put the cooking juice back on the heat and add ½ leaf of gelatine and cook until almost syrup.
- Add this to the carrots in the blender and add 1 tbsp of olive oil.
- Blend until very smooth. Pass through a sieve to remove the seeds of cardamom and any lumpy bits.

Cauliflower fritters with sage

This is great with a dip made of lemon
mayonnaise and a little anchovy paste.

125g flour
175ml beer
1 egg yolk
3 egg whites
2 tbsp sage leaves, finely chopped
salt
1 large cauliflower, cleaned and
divided into florets

- Heat the deep fat tryer to 170°C.
- Sieve the flour and add a pinch of salt.
- Whisk in the beer and egg yolk
  until smooth.
- Add the chopped sage.
- Whisk the egg whites until they are fluffy
  and hold soft peaks.
- Gently fold into the base mixture.
- Put the cauliflower florets in the batter and
  mix well.
- Deep fry them, in small batches, in the hot
  oil until golden brown.

Vegetables

Oven-roasted celeriac with bacon and rosemary

1 large celeriac, peeled and sliced in
to 8-10 parts
½ tbsp lemon thyme, chopped
½ tbsp rosemary, chopped
2 cloves garlic, chopped
2 tbsp olive oil
pepper and sea salt, freshly ground
20 slices streaky bacon

- Pre-heat the oven to 165°C.
- Season the celeriac with pepper and sea salt, then add the chopped lemon thyme , rosemary, garlic and, finally, the olive oil.
- Mix well and leave for 10 minutes.
- Then put two slices of bacon on a baking sheet and wrap them around one of the pieces of celeriac.
- Repeat until all of the celeriac is wrapped in bacon.
- Put in the oven until the bacon is crispy and the celeriac is soft in the middle.

Spinach soufflé

600g spinach, rinsed and the tough stalks
and outer leaves removed
4 egg yolks
10 egg whites
70g butter
80g plain flour
salt and pepper, freshly ground

Makes 10 ramekins (buttered and floured)

- Pre-heat the oven to 160°C.
- Bring 2 litres of water to the boil and season with salt, then add the spinach. Cook until tender and drain.
- Process spinach until smooth.
- Now make a roux with the butter and flour, add the spinach purée and mix well. Use a whisk to remove any lumps.
- Mix in the egg yolks and bring to a soft boil. Pour into a large bowl.
- Whisk the egg whites until they are fluffy and hold soft peaks.
- Gently fold the whites into the spinach base.
- Season the mixture and spoon it into the ramekins to the brim.
- Cook the soufflés for 12 - 14 minutes, until well risen and lightly coloured.

Swiss chard tartare

400g Swiss chard, rinsed and the tough stalks
and outer leaves removed
½ tbsp capers, chopped
½ tbsp gherkins, chopped
½ tbsp shallots, chopped
½ tbsp black olives, chopped
½ tbsp flatleaf parsley, chopped
Salt, pepper to taste
2 cloves of garlic

- Bring 2 litres of water to the boil and season it with salt.
- Add the garlic cloves and cook for 2 minutes.
- Drop in the Swiss chard and cook for 10 seconds, then strain directly.
- Cool in iced water.
- When cooled remove and squeeze out the water.
- Chop the Swiss chard leaves and garlic until fine then add the chopped capers, gherkins, shallots, black olives and the flatleaf parsley. Check for seasoning.

Served on homemade crostini, it makes a perfect match with fish.

Turnip confit with garden thyme

Cooking vegetables in oil confers some benefits. For example, it really does intensify the flavour but as salt cannot dissolve in oil, it has to be added later.

But the key thing is that the flavour molecules stay inside instead of being washed away. Just consider how we normally cook asparagus and how much flavour leaches into the water. No wonder we make soup with it.

You can confit potato, celeriac, pumpkin, cauliflower, carrots and even asparagus. Careful draining and wiping off the oil before serving is essential.

500ml rapeseed oil
½ bunch of thyme
1 clove garlic, crushed
1 tsp peppercorns, crushed
zest of a small orange
1 large turnip, peeled and cut into cubes

- Heat the oil and add the thyme, orange zest, garlic and crushed pepper.
- Then add the turnip cubes and make sure that they are covered by the oil.
- Cook on a very low heat until the turnip is tender.
- Remove from the oil and drain.
- Season with salt and serve.

Vegetables

Potato purée

750g potatoes, peeled
100ml cream
50ml milk
100g butter
salt

- Put the potatoes into a large pot of salted water
- Bring to the boil and cook until the potatoes are tender. Strain.
- Bring the milk, cream and butter to a soft boil.
- Mash the potatoes. Add the hot milk, cream and butter mixture and stir well with a wooden spoon. Season and serve.

It is tempting to leave it at this, but there are other possibilities...

Dairy-free potato purée

Instead of butter, use a rich olive oil and replace the cream and milk with soya milk.

Fresh potato purée

Use creme fraiche instead of cream and olive oil instead of butter.

Potato purée with lemon, pine nuts and rocket

Add to the fresh potato purée the zest of 2 lemons, 90g toasted pine nuts and a finely sliced bunch of rocket leaves. This is very good with fish.

Potato purée with bay leaf and roasted garlic

Replace the butter with bay leaf butter and add garlic purée to taste.

Potato salad with bacon, mustard and chives

500g new potatoes
1 bay leaf, 1 garlic clove, 2 sprigs rosemary,
1 sprig thyme
150g bacon lardons
2 onions, diced
2 tbsp grain mustard
120ml chicken stock
60ml wine vinegar
1 bunch chives
1 tbsp mayonnaise, pepper and salt

- Halve the new potatoes and put them in a pot, just covered with water.
- Add salt and the garlic, bay leaf, rosemary and thyme.
- Bring to the boil, reduce the heat, and gently cook until just done.
- Brown the bacon in a pan.
- Add the onions and stir in the mustard.
- Add the vinegar and bring to the boil. Then add the chicken stock.
- Let the mixture thicken.
- Season and set aside. Slice the chives as thinly as possible.
- Drain the new potatoes and put them in a large bowl.
- Add the bacon mixture, the mayonnaise and the chives.
- Mix well and season.
- Serve the salad warm or cold.

Vegetables

Potato chips or fries

Chips are always difficult. They are never as easy as they look.

A good chip is crisp, golden brown on the outside and soft in the middle. Of course the kind of potato you use is important but also how you cook it and at what temperature.

This is how we do it.

1 kg baking potatoes, peeled and cut into chips of 1.5cm thick – the length does not matter so much.

- Rinse under cold running water for 5 minutes.
- Bring a large pot of salted water to the boil.
- Add the potatoes and bring them to a soft simmer.
- When the chips become tender, carefully remove from the water, drain and let them cool.
- Put in the fridge for an hour.
- Heat the deep fat fryer to 140°C.
- Fry your chips until they start to colour.
- Turn the fryer up to 185°C and fry them until golden brown.

Sprinkle with salt and serve directly.

Fondant potato

8 medium large potatoes
2 garlic cloves, chopped
sprig of thyme and of rosemary
malt vinegar
rapeseed oil
200ml chicken stock

- Pre-heat the oven to 170°C.
- Trim the potatoes down until they are oval-shaped and all equal in size.
- Heat the oil in a heavy pan and cook the potatoes until they are nicely browned.
- Add the garlic, the herbs and a good splash of vinegar.
- Season with salt and add the chicken stock.
- Transfer to an ovenproof tray and put in the oven for 40 minutes, shaking the tray every 5 minutes.
- The potatoes will get an attractive glaze from the stock.

Red cabbage

500g red cabbage, finely sliced
250ml red wine
1 grated apple
1 fresh bay leaf
½ tsp ground cloves
½ fresh nutmeg, grated
½ cinnamon stick
½ onion, finely diced
1 tbsp butter
sugar and salt

- Mix all the ingredients together, except sugar, salt and butter, and put in a saucepan.
- Put on a low heat and stir frequently.
- When the cabbage is tender, taste and add sugar and salt.
- Finish with a small knob of butter.

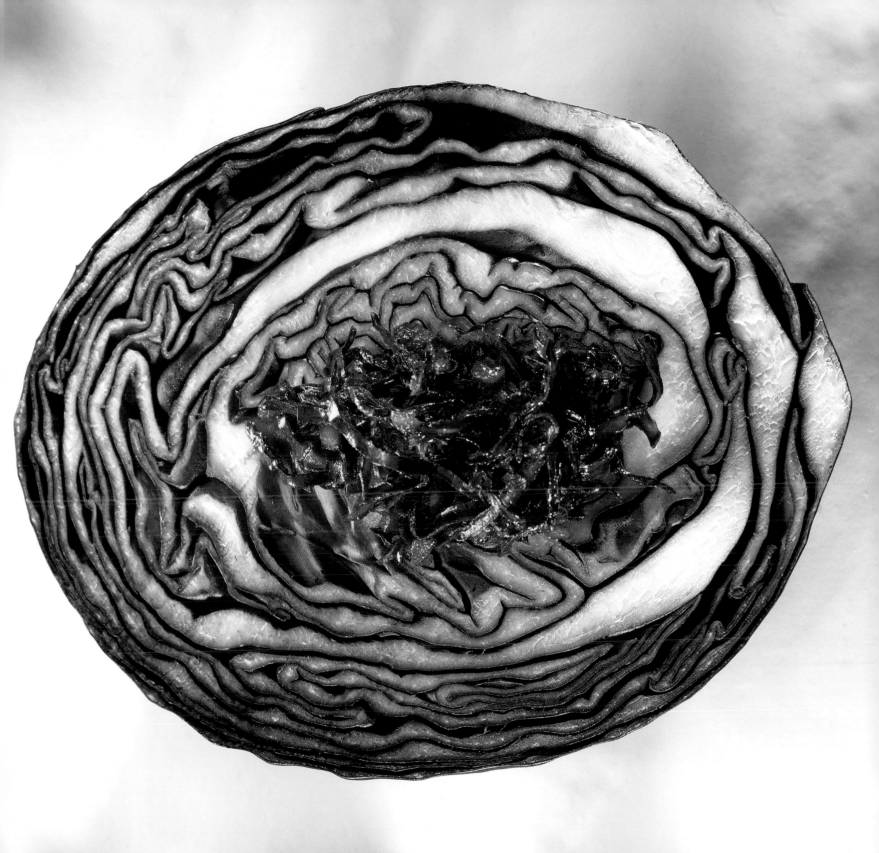

Confit of baby artichokes

Ingredients

20 baby artichokes

¼ bunch of rosemary

¼ bunch of thyme

2 bay leaves

10 black peppercorns, crushed

rapeseed oil

We use globe artichokes throughout the year at The Cliff House. The peak season is, of course, early summer but the harvest carries on. However, we need to preserve artichokes to keep us going through the winter.

We do this by cleaning and trimming them and cooking these delicate vegetables in vacuum bags with oil, herbs and spices at 85°C. At this temperature they keep their structure, flavour and colour.

Artichokes come in different varieties but they tend not to have specific names. We like the ones that can be picked when they are very small and eaten whole, the choke and all.

They are great in a vegetable salad and lovely deep-fried and served with a crisp vinaigrette dressing. Grilled they go very well with roast beef. And they are fine on their own, just warmed through in a white butter sauce.

You can also employ modern technology to cook artichokes; here is how we do it.

A thermometer is invaluable here.

- Trim the stalks to 0.5cm.

- Cut the top 2.5cm off each artichoke.

- Remove the leaves until you get to the light green inside ones.

- Place the artichokes in a pot and cover them with rapeseed oil.

- Add the herbs and pepper.

- Then put on a low heat and bring the temperature to 85°C.

- Let the artichokes simmer in the oil until the leaves can be pulled off easily; this will take about 35 - 45 minutes.

- If you want to preserve them put them in a jar, cover with oil and seal.

- Or else just strain the oil (it can be used again) and let the artichokes cool.

Crispy salsify

with parsley hollandaise

Ingredients

4 salsify roots, peeled and cooked in salted water until tender

1 bunch parsley, stalks removed, chopped, washed and dried

150g breadcrumbs

2 eggs

200g melted butter

50g parsley purée (parsley blended in the food processor with a little olive oil until smooth)

2 egg yolks

50ml white wine vinegar, simmered with bay leaves and black pepper

pepper and salt for seasoning

Salsify is sometimes called the vegetable oyster because some people can detect a mineral-like, oystery kind of flavour in it. In Holland it's called poor man's asparagus but I don't think that name does it justice.

You rarely see salsify for sale, so we have to organise our own supply. The team at St Raphael's grow it for us and we harvest them before the roots get too big. I think they are at their best when they are about 20 cm long and as thick as your forefinger.

You need to be quick or clever (or both) to peel and prepare salsify because it discolours very quickly when its flesh is in contact with the air. The best way to get around this problem is to use a bowl of water to which you have added a dash of vinegar and a good pinch of salt. Peel the roots as quickly as you can and sink them into this bath.

This deep-fried version is a wonderful pre-dinner snack and it shows how well parsley and salsify enhance each other. It tastes beautiful and looks great. In fact, root vegetables have never looked so good. And it's particularly good to serve with oysters, by the way.

- Mix the breadcrumbs and the parsley together and spread out on a baking tray to dry.

- Cut the salsify into evenly sized pieces (15 cm or longer), then flour them lightly.

- Break the eggs into a bowl and mix well.

- Dip the salsify pieces in the egg mixture and coat them with the parsley crumbs. You will need to do this twice to get the right thickness.

- Fill a pot with water and place on a high heat. When the water boils, turn the heat down to a gentle simmer.

- In a large mixing bowl mix the egg yolks with the white wine vinegar. Then place the bowl above the simmering water and beat the mixture until it has a fluffy and creamy texture.

- Remove from the heat and start adding the melted butter, drop by drop, as if you were making mayonnaise, whisking all the time. When all the butter is absorbed, fold in the parsley purée and adjust the seasoning.

- Deep-fry the salsify until crisp.

- Pour the parsley hollandaise into a tumbler until one third full and place three of the salsify pieces on top.

Chef's vegetable salad

Ingredients

12 cauliflower rosettes, blanched and marinated with tarragon and some almond oil

8 baby turnips, cooked in organic apple juice with sea salt

8 baby carrots, cooked in 300ml vegetable stock with 1 tbsp sugar and 1 tbsp of vinegar until almost done, then left to cool in this sweet and sour stock

8 asparagus tips, pan-fried in grapeseed oil until just cooked

4 white radishes, thinly sliced

2 red beetroot, roasted whole in sea salt, then peeled, sliced and seasoned

8 celeriac cubes, cooked in olive oil with apple mint

4 baby courgettes with their flowers, deep-fried in batter (see page 57)

4 baby artichokes, slowly cooked in vegetable stock with lemon balm

10 broccoli rosettes, boiled in salted water, then puréed in a blender with a little olive oil, seasoning and orange zest

2 parsnips, boiled in salted water, puréed in a blender with some hazelnuts and parsley

4 garlic cloves, slowly cooked in olive oil and then deep-fried in batter

8 spring onions, blanched and grilled on the barbecue with nasturtium oil

80g small tomatoes, sliced and marinated with basil, sea salt and oil

My eldest son calls me the vegetable policeman and he has a point. Vegetables are important in my kitchen, not just because I love them but also because they are the most versatile raw materials.

To highlight this I came up with a vegetable salad that reflects the season at a particular time. It's always changing, and it can contain more than twenty different ingredients, all prepared in different ways from grilled to raw, from marinated to fried. This is so much a playground of textures, colours and flavours that it makes the ultimate starter. Even for non-vegetarians.

This dish is not mine. It's everyone's because it's all about the person who is putting it together, the mood, the season, what the weather is like. It reflects the feel of the moment. It's the naked truth.

Anyway, this is just a guideline as to how to compose your vegetable salad.

Several dried vegetables: leeks, red onion, asparagus, carrot.

Several fresh herbs and flowers: chives, chervil, cress, nasturtium, borage, sage.

Several different oils: horseradish, lemon, and parsley.

Arrange the dish to your liking, maybe on a large platter.

Heritage tomato collection

This salad is hugely popular on our tasting menu and comes as a very pleasant surprise after the main course, refreshing and cleansing the palate in readiness for the last two dessert courses. The other surprise, for most people, is eating tomatoes that actually taste of something. Modern supermarket tomatoes are just water.

This salad performs a really valuable function in the construction of the tasting menu. And I often think that chefs don't give enough thought to the order in which courses are served. I mean, it's crazy to start a meal

with duck liver paté or foie gras. This means you start the meal with the element that is hardest to digest. I think duck liver paté or foie gras should be served instead of cheese! But who am I to dictate? Anyway, there are no rules, just common sense.

The old and unusual varieties of tomato that are no longer grown by the big commercial producers are known as heirloom tomatoes in the US while here we tend to call them heritage varieties. Not that it makes any difference. It's the taste and the character and the textures and the colours that matter. The actual ingredients depend, simply, on what is ripe in our own garden and at St Raphael's. The composition varies from day to day and week to week. That, and the intensity of flavour, make it an exciting dish.

And so, this is not a recipe. Just a list of suggestions as to what you mix together and serve, however elegantly or inelegantly as you like. Here goes...

Ingredients

Cherry tomato - cured and dried

Green Zebra - raw but marinated with lemon oil and basil

Red Pear - injected with rosemary and black pepper

Brandywine- juiced and made in to a jelly with watermelon

Tigerella - grilled

Purple Plum - dried in chips

Yellow Pear - just on its own

Purple Kabash - sorbet

Fresh herbs and flowers from the garden

Lemon zest, Maldon sea salt, arbequina olive oil

Warm tomato salad

Ingredients

8 ripe plum tomatoes

200g Ardsallagh soft goat's cheese

75g rocket leaves

30g toasted pinenuts

zest of 1 lemon

malt vinegar

rapeseed oil, black pepper and sea salt

The wonderful people at the St Raphael's Centre in Youghal have a big garden with two large greenhouses where they grow twelve different varieties of heirloom tomatoes for us. It's amazing to see this Mediterranean vegetable, or fruit to be precise, thriving in this part of Ireland.

These are tomatoes that go back a long way. They are no longer in large scale commercial production because they don't store well enough for the supermarket trade. But they have interesting shapes, colours and flavours. And the flavours are really intense. They taste of the past.

The varieties we use include Green Zebra, Yellow Pear, Brandywine, Purple Kabash, Costoluto Fiorentino, Tigerella and Red Cherry. Even the names tell you how different they are.

You can't judge the ripeness of a tomato by smelling it. The only way is to feel it and look at the colour. If it's somewhere between firm and soft and the skin has a good shine, it is ready to be eaten. Don't keep your tomatoes in the fridge. Keep them and eat them at room temperature.

If you have really good tomatoes like the ones we enjoy at The Cliff House, you won't want to do too much to them. Just pick them and give them a wash. Then slice and put them on a plate with a drizzle of olive oil, black pepper, sea salt and maybe a little bit of lemon zest. Like this, they are just fantastic, but if you want to add something extra you can try fresh goat's cheese with basil leaves and toasted almonds. Or serve with grilled mackerel.

This is a recipe with plum tomatoes where we grill them and serve with fresh rocket, local soft goat's cheese and pinenuts.

- Pre-heat the grill pan.

- Halve the tomatoes and sprinkle with rapeseed oil and sea salt.

- Grill them cut side down until they are marked, then turn them.

- Add 3 tbsp of malt vinegar to the grill pan.

- Put the grilled tomatoes on a plate and put goat's cheese on top.

- Add pepper and lemon zest and pour over the vinegar.

- Sprinkle with pinenuts and dress with the rocket leaves.

- Serve.

Grilled fennel salad

with blood orange, watercress and Ardsallagh goat's cheese

Ingredients

6 fennel bulbs

2 blood oranges

100g Ardsallagh hard goat's cheese

75g watercress

70ml olive oil

25ml white wine vinegar

black pepper, coarse sea salt

This is a great healthy late autumn salad with lots of flavour and texture. There's the peppery crispness of watercress, the sweet acidity of the first blood oranges, and the creamy tang of the goat's cheese. And of course the spiciness of the fennel.

When buying fennel make sure that they are small, white, fresh and that they smell properly of aniseed. This salad can be prepared in advance and be served either warm or cold.

- Remove the fennel leaves and put in a bowl with the oil and vinegar.

- Add zest of half an orange and a pinch of salt.

- Blend to a smooth dressing and set aside.

- Bring a large pan of salted water to the boil.

- Cut the fennel bulbs into quarters and cook in the salted water until tender.

- Remove from the pan and sprinkle with oil and sea salt.

- Grill the fennel on all sides under a pre-heated grill.

- While still hot, marinate in the dressing and add the zest of the other half of the orange. Set aside.

- Remove the skin of the remaining orange and slice the flesh into thin segments.

- Arrange three fennel quarters on each plate and arrange the segments of orange around them.

- Divide the goat's cheese between the four plates.

- Drizzle with the dressing and grind pepper over.

- Arrange the watercress on each plate and serve.

Tomato explosion

Okay, this may seem a bit weird but it really does work. And it's one of those things that make cooking - and eating - more fun. I like creating surprises when I cook. But I also like to retain the true identity of the flavours with which I am working.

It is a very simple concept. I came up with this idea when I was making ketchup. It just struck me that drying a whole small tomato will concentrate flavour, and then, if you add the right liquid it becomes a kind of embodiment of ketchup ketchup in the shape of a tomato!

The nice thing about being the chef is that you don't have to submit your ideas for approval by a committee. If it seems like a good one, you just do it.

Tomato explosion makes a great party snack. I have even made a virtual Bloody Mary this way with celery salt and a vodka infusion. This is how you do it. Give it a try.

- Take small cherry tomatoes and with a toothpick make a few small holes in them.

- Dry in a dehydrator overnight.

- From the ketchup recipe we take all the ingredients except the tomatoes.

- From these ingredients we make a syrup by boiling them together until the mixture thickens

- Put the syrup in a small pipette.

- Inject a little into each semi-dried tomato.

Ingredients

Small cherry tomatoes

200ml vinegar

3 onions, chopped

2 celery stalks, chopped

2 hot peppers, seeds removed, chopped

1 red pepper, seeds removed, chopped

50g grated fresh ginger

1 tbsp mustard

½ tbsp ground star anise and cloves

3 cloves garlic, finely chopped

250g brown sugar

Green peas

Ingredients

200g cleaned fresh garden peas, podded

½ bunch oregano

zest of 1 lemon

2 tbsp olive oil

seasoning

We grow our own peas. It's the only way to capture the truly fresh taste that so many people know nothing about. Chefs have no idea how much trouble peas involve. The amount of time that harvesting the pea crop takes is amazing and it's a job that requires real precision. And then there's the podding to be done. I get our chefs on to this job during the season, just to make sure that they always have a full appreciation of peas.

And so, they treat the vegetable with more respect. Actually, that's our policy with all of the fruit and vegetables and herbs at The Cliff House. We get the people who cook into direct contact with the produce, the garden, the harvest. Some chefs think that fresh produce comes out of the back of a van. Our guys know better.

Peas are so common in Ireland that we sometimes spoil them. As one of the ubiquitous "meat and three veg", as mushy peas with fish and chips, overcooked in soups. This recipe elevates peas to the status they deserve - but only if they are just picked and freshly podded.

- Put plenty of salted water (as salty as the sea) in a big pot and bring to the boil.

- Add the peas to the boiling water.

- Boil for 2 minutes and drain.

- Mix together fresh pepper, the oregano leaves, 2 tbsp olive oil and lemon zest.

- Toss the hot peas with this mixture and serve directly, either with grilled lamb or on their own.

- You can always use a blender and make the best mushy peas from the remainder!

Bread and butter pudding

with wild mushrooms

Ingredients

20 slices of white or brown bread,
crusts removed

500g wild mushrooms

500ml milk

200ml cream

1 garlic clove, crushed

1 tsp rosemary, chopped

½ tsp thyme, chopped

7 egg yolks

1 tbsp truffle oil

butter

seasoning

12 x 20 cm baking tray lined
with greaseproof paper

Ireland has an abundance of wild mushrooms and because a lot of people are afraid of picking something poisonous they don't get devastated like they do in France or Russia. We have a local forager who supplies us from the area around Ardmore and, I would guess, from the woodlands that sweep down to the River Blackwater near Youghal. He really knows his stuff and naturally he keeps the best mushroom sites very carefully to himself. All mushroom hunters have secrets!

As a child I loved to eat baked mushrooms with garlic on toast. This is one of those things you learn at catering school that stay with you for life.

Just to be a little bit different, we make a savoury bread and butter pudding with wild mushrooms and the combination is just right. The bread absorbs the mushroom juices and holds the flavour well, while the contrast between the soft interior and the crisp outside of the pudding is fabulous.

This is a good vegetarian supper dish or an amazing accompaniment to something else. The best thing is that it is very simple to make at home if you can get the right kind of mushrooms.

- Pre-heat the oven to 170°C.

- Butter the bread slices.

- Mix the egg yolks and truffle oil, cream, milk, garlic, rosemary, thyme together and season.

- Put a layer of buttered bread in the baking tray.

- Cover with a layer of mushrooms.

- Then put another layer of buttered bread on top.

- Pour the liquid mixture on top and press it down.

- Bake in the oven for 40 minutes.

- Leave it to cool and cut into serving portions.

- Bake for a further 10 minutes at 180°C and serve, perhaps with some baked mushrooms and herbs.

Cold sauces

A lot of chefs think that a dish without a sauce is not a dish at all.
As it happens, I don't agree but, of course, I'm a romantic.

A lot of chefs think that a dish without a sauce is not a dish at all. As it happens, I don't agree but, of course, I'm a romantic. I believe that some dishes are complete in themselves and can't be improved. In fact, they can be spoiled if you make additions.

Essentially what I'm saying is that if you decide to serve a sauce, think first and be sure that it's both a good one and appropriate to what you are serving it with.

The thing that worries me most about sauces is how they can be used to cover the truth of a dish, the real flavour. Sometimes the effect will be to hide the true character of the dish and you lose something important; and sometimes sauces are used to disguise inferior raw materials. This is simply wrong.

At The Cliff House, we always ensure that sauces truly complement the dishes with which they are served. Otherwise the dish becomes just a garnish for the sauce!

These are just guidelines as to how to make sauces. Use your own ingenuity, taste and sense of adventure and build your own versions from these basics.

Basic mayonnaise

240ml groundnut oil
1 egg yolk
1½ tsp mustard
½ tsp Worcestershire Sauce
2 tsp vinegar or lemon juice
salt and pepper

- Put the egg yolk, mustard, Worcestershire Sauce, vinegar and seasoning in a mixing bowl.
- Whisk until smooth.
- Drop by drop, whisk in the oil until a smooth, thick mixture is achieved.
- Should the mayonnaise split, just add 1 tbsp of hot water and start whisking from the side to the middle and the mayonnaise will start to emulsify again.
- Keep the mayonnaise in the fridge.

Tartare sauce

150ml basic mayonnaise
1 tbsp gherkins, chopped
1 tbsp capers, chopped
1 tbsp parsley, chopped
1 tbsp chives, finely chopped
zest of ½ lemon

- Mix all ingredients together, season to taste and serve.

Marie-Rose sauce

200ml basic mayonnaise
50ml tomato ketchup
½ tbsp Irish whiskey
½ tbsp dry sherry
1 tsp ginger syrup
½ tsp ground paprika

- Dissolve the ground paprika in the ginger syrup.
- Add the mayonnaise and the tomato ketchup and mix.
- Stir in the whiskey and the sherry and season to taste.

Scallion and ham mayonnaise

200ml basic mayonnaise
½ bunch of scallions, sliced in rings
50g ham, finely diced
1 tbsp parsley, chopped
zest of ½ lemon

- Mix all ingredients together, season to taste and serve.

Use your own ingenuity, taste and sense of adventure and build your own versions from these basics.

Lemon and horseradish mayonnaise

200ml basic mayonnaise
50g horseradish, freshly grated
zest of 2 lemons and juice of 1 lemon

- Mix all ingredients together, season to taste and serve.

Green mayonnaise (for salads and grilled dishes)

200ml basic mayonnaise
50g watercress or parsley

- Put the watercress or parsley into a blender.
- Add 2 tbsp of mayonnaise and blend.
- When the mixture goes green and smooth, add the rest of the mayonnaise and serve.

Mustard and honey mayonnaise (for barbecued dishes and pork)

200ml basic mayonnaise
2 tbsp grain mustard
1 tbsp honey

- Mix all ingredients together, season to taste and serve.

Green herb sauce

3 tbsp parsley, finely chopped
2 tbsp tarragon, finely chopped
2 tbsp chives, finely chopped
2 tbsp chervil, finely chopped
2 tbsp basil, finely sliced
2 tbsp dill or fennel leaf, finely chopped
1 tbsp mint, finely chopped
1 tbsp capers, finely chopped
1 tbsp anchovies, finely chopped
1 tbsp garlic, finely chopped
1 tbsp mustard
250ml olive oil
zest and juice of 1 lemon
freshly ground pepper and salt

Mix everything together and serve with roasted potatoes, grilled fish, meat, poultry, vegetables and salads. It doesn't matter how you use it, it just lifts virtually every dish. You can also put this mixture in a blender and make it into a lovely green paste.

Aïoli

5 garlic cloves
2 egg yolks
300ml olive oil
salt and pepper
½ lemon

- Crush the fresh garlic and add to the egg yolks.
- Season with salt and pepper and add the juice of half a lemon.
- Whisk until smooth.
- Drop by drop, whisk in the oil until a smooth, thick, emulsified mixture is achieved.
- Serve with toasted bread, salads, fish or raw vegetables.

Seafood

Garnished oysters

Ingredients

24 oysters

1 bunch of chives, finely chopped

3 shallots, finely diced

3 lemons

80ml cider vinegar

black pepper

crushed ice

Ireland and oysters just seem to go together. The clean, cold waters of the Atlantic coastline are where these marine creatures feel very much at home.

They should be eaten only when there is an R in the month. We ignore them for the rest of the year because, as they are breeding, the texture is just not right. People describe it as "milky" and it gives you some idea of what is involved. Oysters, at their best, are dense, salty, slippery and tasting intensely of the sea. You really should not compromise.

The coastline between Youghal and Dungarvan is called Helvick, after Helvick Head. Ardmore is right in the middle of

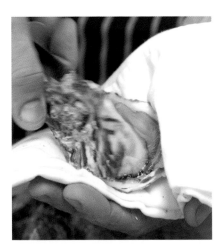

it and only a stone's throw from The Cliff House Hotel we found a man farming Helvick oysters. The strange thing is that it took a Dutchman to serve these local oysters in the locality!

Maybe too many people believe that produce from far away is somehow more exotic, more interesting. But they are very wrong. Almost 95% of Helvick oysters go for export, to places like France where they are really appreciated. We account for a lot of the rest.

When eating oysters, keep it very, very simple.

- Open the oysters.

- Strain the juices and replace the oysters in their shells.

- Add a little of the juices to the oysters.

- Halve the lemons and sear them on a hot plate until caramelised; then wrap them in muslin, tied with string.

- Divide the chives and shallots between four glasses.

- Arrange the oysters on the crushed ice.

- On a separate board serve the garnish: cider vinegar, chives, black pepper, shallots and lemon.

Oysters with Guinness

blackcurrant and hazelnut

Ingredients

24 oysters

100ml Guinness stout

100ml blackcurrant coulis

½ leaf of gelatine

sea salt

10ml hazelnut oil

50g hazelnuts, skinned

lemon zest

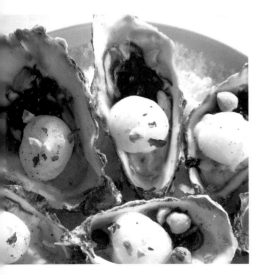

I'm one of those people who believe that if you come to Ireland you have to drink stout. After all, Guinness is the *vin de pays* here. The trouble is, I have to admit that I'm not really a Guinness fancier, having been brought up on Dutch beer. Now, there's a real contrast of styles.

However, when in Rome... At the pub in Ardmore I still have the odd pint of Guinness but the barman has made my life a bit easier by adding a dash of blackcurrant cordial. Okay, so the guys at the bar tend to laugh at me; this is not a proper man's way to drink stout, but what the hell?

Just after I got introduced to the pleasures of Guinness with "a dash of black" as it's cryptically called in these parts, I went to Dublin and visited a farmers' market where, at nine o'clock in the morning, they were eating oysters with a mouthful of Guinness. My motto is try before you die, and you know what? It was magic. There is something about this classic Irish combination that is just luscious.

It gave me an idea to combine the oysters, Guinness and blackcurrant, with some crunch from hazelnuts. It was my first Irish recipe.

- Open the oysters.

- Strain and replace the oysters in their shells. Reserve the juice.

- Bring blackcurrant coulis to a simmer. Season with salt and pepper.

- Then dissolve the gelatine in the coulis and bring to the boil.

- When it thickens, strain into a bowl.

- Cool, and when the jelly is set, cover it until needed.

- Put a non-stick pan on a medium heat. Add the hazelnuts and toss until golden brown.

- Toss with hazelnut oil and sea salt.

- Then add a teaspoon of stout to each oyster.

- Place half a teaspoon of blackcurrant jelly on each oyster.

- Sprinkle with the toasted hazelnuts and lemon zest.

Photograph shows this dish with oyster "meringue" as served at The Cliff House.

Shrimps in sea salt

Ingredients

2 kg shrimps (in the shell)

3 kg coarse sea salt

3 egg whites

Seaweed from the beach,
washed thoroughly

Lemon mayonnaise

2 egg yolks

2 lemons

1 tsp mustard

500ml rapeseed oil

Shrimps are for sharing. You just cook them, put them in a big bowl on the table and sit around it and chat and peel away. I don't understand the psychology of it, but there's something about sharing food like this that's amazingly relaxing. Try it and experience for yourself the great conversation and the laughter.

What I'm suggesting in this dish is almost too simple to be true. You need only sea salt, fresh shrimps and lemon mayonnaise.

- Pre-heat the oven to 200°C.

- Put the sea salt, egg whites and a dash of water in a large mixing bowl.

- Mix together until you have a soggy mass.

- Roughly chop the seaweed and add to the salt mixture.

- Spread a small part of the mixture on a baking tray.

- Lay the shrimps on top.

- Cover completely with the rest of the sea salt mixture.

- Bake for 25 minutes.

- In the meantime, make the mayonnaise.

- Put the egg yolks, juice of 1 lemon, the mustard and a pinch of salt in a clean mixing bowl and whisk until combined.

- Whisk in the oil, drop by drop.

- Then add the zest of 2 lemons and season to taste with pepper and salt.

- Put the tray on the table and break open the salt crust to reveal the shrimps.

- Peel and dip the shrimps in the mayonnaise and have fun!

Shrimp balls

When the tide is at its lowest, I go out with my family to catch shrimps from around Ardmore Bay. It was my wife who discovered this little fun activity and my sons, Tygo and Floyd, are very keen shrimp hunters.

When we've got our haul, the shrimps are taken home and cooked. We then eat them on toast with a wee bit of mayonnaise and a twist of pepper. It's a real treat.

I serve them at The Cliff House as well. Here they are cooked, peeled and then transformed into the most delicious shrimp snack, the "bitterbal", as we call it in Dutch. This means that we make a very thick ragout with shrimp stock and peeled shrimps, and coat dollops of this with breadcrumbs and deep fry. It's luscious.

- Melt butter and add the flour; stir with a wooden spoon until it comes together as a little ball.

- When it no longer sticks to the bottom of the pan, the mixture is cooked.

- Add milk and the prawn stock and stir until there are no lumps.

- Bring to a soft boil and let it simmer for 30 minutes.

- Soak the gelatine leaves in cold water.

- After 30 minutes dissolve the gelatine in the mixture.

- Then add the shrimps, zest of the lemon and the parsley.

- Season to taste and pour on to a tray. Let it cool in the fridge for at least 2 hours.

- Spread some flour on a tray.

- Make 4cm balls from the refrigerated mixture and roll them through the flour.

- Put in the freezer for 2 hours.

- Whisk the eggs with salt and spread the breadcrumbs on a tray.

- Carefully dip the balls into the egg and then coat them with the breadcrumbs.

- After the first coating, repeat the process once more.

- Keep the shrimp balls in the fridge or freeze them right away.

- Deep-fry at 175°C until golden brown.

Ingredients

250ml milk

250ml prawn stock/vegetable stock

80g butter

90g flour

500g shrimps, peeled

15g gelatine leaves

zest of 1 lemon

2 tbsp flatleaf parsley

pepper and sea salt

500g breadcrumbs

2 eggs

flour

Prawns with parsley and lemon

Ingredients

12 whole Dublin Bay prawns per person

olive oil

1 bunch of parsley, stalks removed

1 lemon

½ garlic clove

2 anchovy fillets

olive oil, sea salt, black pepper

Prawns are fragile and they have a tendency to shrink And so they are best cooked in their shells. It's best to butterfly them, i.e. cut them down the middle but not all the way through, so that they can be opened out and cooked flat.

The amount of parsley growing in our garden reflects its importance in the kitchen. We grow both the traditional curly variety that everyone remembers from old-fashioned butcher's shops and the Continental flatleaf kind. The curly one has a great, deep, earthy flavour while the flatleaf sort is really pungent.

We partner the flatleaf parsley with our local Helvick prawns to produce a great explosion of flavour. Green herb sauce (see page 85) is another good accompaniment.

- Cut the prawns lengthwise and clean the heads.

- Put a little salt in a mortar and pestle with the garlic and the anchovies.

- Rub to a smooth paste, adding the parsley little by little together with some olive oil.

- Keep doing this until all the parsley is incorporated.

- Add the juice and zest of the lemon and season.

- Sear the prawns meat side down in a very hot pan until the edges go golden brown.

- Place the prawns on each plate, meat side up.

- Spoon the parsley paste over the prawns and serve.

Prawns with nasturtium cakes

and salad leaves

Ingredients

500g potatoes, peeled and cubed

1 tbsp chives, chopped

1 tbsp shallots, chopped

1 tbsp grated lemon zest

1 clove garlic, chopped

3 tbsp nasturtium leaves, chopped

pepper and sea salt, freshly ground

20 large prawns, peeled

lemon juice

olive oil

1 bowl mixed salad leaves (tarragon, flatleaf parsley, chives, wild fennel, rocket, nasturtium flowers, borage flowers, sage)

Prawns, or langoustines, are simply a source of joy for a chef. When they are good - and we get some of the best here in Ardmore - you could not wish for better raw materials, so packed with wonderful taste. This is chefs' gold.

Dublin Bay prawns don't come from Dublin Bay. This is just the name given to this species of crustacean. Our Dublin Bay prawns, strange as it may seem, come from off Helvick Head in West Waterford. And we reckon they beat anything that comes out of Dublin Bay!

Chefs always want them alive, as it's the ultimate guarantee of freshness but there's a catch. If you get them alive, they are impossible to peel. I get around this by getting live prawns and letting them stand for a while.

A further problem is that the white blood cells stay alive in the prawn after death and produce ammonia. This means that the prawns appear to go off very quickly (which is something that happens with skate or ray too). If we peel the prawns we do this in the walk-in fridge so as to keep them as cool as possible. It's not a very popular job!

The shells can be used to make very flavourful oils, sauces or powders.

The potato cakes are made with nasturtium because this really works with the prawns and it gives a very distinctive kick. Nasturtium tastes a little like capers but if you don't have any you can always substitute watercress or rocket. It won't taste the same but it will give a bit of a kick, and that's what you want.

- Bring 2 litres of salted water to the boil and add the potatoes.

- Drain when cooked.

- Mash the potatoes, then add the olive oil, chopped chives, chopped shallots, grated lemon zest, chopped garlic, and chopped nasturtium; season to taste.

- Leave to cool, and then make small round cakes of the potato mixture.

- Fry them on a medium heat until golden and crisp.

- Sprinkle the prawns with olive oil and roast in a non-stick pan.

- Mix the salad leaves with freshly ground pepper, sea salt, lemon juice and olive oil.

- Put a nasturtium cake in the centre of each plate, place the prawns on top and surround with the salad mixture.

Fish and chips

Ingredients

4 fillets of fresh fish
(200g without the skin)

100g flour

2 eggs

500g fresh breadcrumbs

1 tbsp chopped parsley,
tarragon and mint each

zest of 1 lemon

seasoning

When it comes to fish and chips, there's only one thing that matters: freshness, that's the sole criterion. At The Cliff House, we choose the fish for our fish and chips that we serve on the bar menu purely on the basis of what is best on the day.

Our fishmonger's delivery dictates whether it's to be pollock or plaice, haddock or hake, gurnard or cod.

In Ireland, the tradition is to cook fish in batter but I feel that this can be too heavy and fatty. I prefer to use breadcrumbs because somehow they seem lighter and you get a greater sense of the taste of the fish, which is what it should be all about.

And the chips must be crisp but fluffy inside, the perfect match for the fish.

This is our version of a humble classic.

- Heat the oil in a deep fat fryer to 165°C.

- Season the fish fillets generously with pepper and salt.

- Mix the breadcrumbs with the chopped herbs (or leave out the herbs if you prefer).

- Whisk the eggs with an eggcup of water and a pinch of salt.

- Coat the fish in a thin layer of flour.

- Then coat the fish thoroughly with the egg mixture.

- Then place the fish in the breadcrumbs, pressing softly.

- Repeat this process of egg and breadcrumbs once more.

- Make sure that the whole fish is thoroughly coated.

- Deep-fry the fish until crisp and brown. Depending on the thickness it will take between 4 and 6 minutes.

- When cooked, sprinkle with salt and lemon zest.

- Serve with chips (see page 62) and tartare sauce (see page 82), and a mixed salad.

Salad of slow-cooked lobster

with turnip cream and tarragon

Lobster has a nasty habit of getting tough and chewy if you overcook it – even slightly. We avoid this by slowly poaching the lobster in a very aromatic herb stock that is perfect for fish or shellfish.

In this salad we use a vegetable that I always associate with Ireland, the turnip. This is what I think of as a character vegetable of the first order. It has sweet, earthy and bitter flavours with great depth.

Tarragon is a really important element in this dish so make sure you include it. Tarragon thrives in our garden and I use it lavishly in the kitchen.

- Heat rapeseed oil in a medium-sized pot and add the fennel, celery and shallots.

- Then add the herbs, a teaspoon of all the dried spices and the vinegar.

- Bring the vinegar to the boil and add 900ml water.

- Let it simmer for 10 minutes and season with sea salt.

- Now put the lobsters in a similarly sized pot, off the heat, and pour the boiling stock on top.

- Let the lobsters cool down in this. They will cook very, very slowly.

- After 1 hour remove the lobsters and clean them.

- Prepare the turnip cream by dicing the turnip into small cubes.

- Boil the turnip in the vegetable stock with seasoning.

- When cooked, strain and purée in a blender with the olive oil to a smooth cream.

- Season to taste and add some grated lemon zest.

- Blend the basic vinaigrette with a few tarragon leaves.

- Put a few dots of the cream on the plate and place the tail and the claw around these. Arrange a few lettuce leaves around it with some julienne of apple, crushed hazelnuts and tarragon leaves. The vinaigrette can be drizzled on the lobster meat together with some ground black pepper and sea salt.

Ingredients

Lobsters

2 Irish lobsters

1 fennel bulb, very finely diced

4 celery stalks, very finely diced

2 shallots, very finely diced

40g tarragon, parsley, chervil, dill, mint – stalks only, no leaves

100ml vinegar

sea salt

rapeseed oil

1 tsp peppercorns, coriander seeds, fennel seeds each

Turnip Cream

250g turnip

200ml vegetable stock

40ml olive oil

sea salt, lemon zest

Garnish/dressing

50ml basic vinaigrette

½ bunch tarragon

½ butterhead lettuce

1 apple, sliced in julienne strips

30g hazelnuts, crushed

Lobster with roasted bone marrow

Ingredients

8 large marrow bones

olive oil, sea salt,
rosemary, garlic

1 cooked lobster
(see Slow-cooked lobster, page 103)

4 slices white bread

2 tbsp parsley, chopped

1 tbsp capers, chopped

1 tbsp shallots, sliced

1 garlic clove, finely chopped

Bone marrow is a real delicacy but it has almost died out. The classic way to eat it is with parsley and garlic on toast and it's always a delicious reminder that you can use almost every part of the animal.

Bone marrow is incredibly easy to prepare and is absolutely packed with flavour. Some people worry about catching BSE from bone marrow but there's no evidence whatsoever that there is any risk. A lot of other people are just a bit squeamish about eating the inside of bones and this is probably because we've all become too well-off and unadventurous. Marrow bones are cheap; in some cases they are free; frugal has never tasted so good.

When we put this dish on the menu it was a great hit with a lot of customers but others were very wary. You could see they really wanted the lobster but the marrow was just a bridge too far. Which was a shame, because it's fabulous. And it doesn't even have to be lobster. Prawns, shrimps or crab will do just as well.

- Heat the oven to 170°C.

- Chop the rosemary and garlic very finely.

- Mix with 2-3 tbsp olive oil and cover the marrow bones with it.

- Sprinkle sea salt on the top, and roast until the bone marrow is soft - 25-30 minutes.

- Clean the lobster and slice the meat into medallions or cubes.

- Cut the bread into cubes.

- Mix with the lobster, parsley, capers, shallots and garlic.

- Scrape the marrow out of the bones, chop roughly and combine with the bread mixture.

- Put into the hollow centres of the bones.

- Roast at 200°C for 12 minutes.

- Serve on its own with mixed salad and toasted bread.

Seafood

Grilled lobster

with garlic, honey and lemon

At The Cliff House we serve lobster that has not travelled far. In fact it has hardly travelled at all because it's caught by our friend Mr Cronin, using his little boat and his few lobster pots, right below the hotel in Ardmore Bay. He has been catching lobster here for over 40 years.

For me, the most exquisite way to eat lobster is straight off the barbecue. The smoky flavour from the hot charcoal combined with that sweet, salty tang of lobster adds to a perfume that is much, much better then Chanel No. 5!

Grilled lobster is great with lemon and mayonnaise and maybe a crunchy salad.

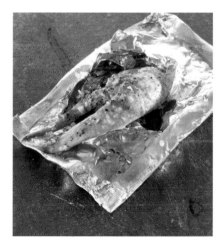

- Boil the lobsters in a big pot of salted water: it will take 1 minute for every 100g.

- Then rinse them in cold water to stop the cooking process.

- Then clean the lobster by halving it lengthways and removing the guts.

- Crack the claws and elbows open with a lobster cracker.

- Brush the lobster halves with the garlic oil and sprinkle with honey.

- Marinate the lobster claws with a bit of olive oil, lemon zest and pepper, then fold into aluminium foil and make a small packet

- Grill the lobster halves, meat side down, until brown, then put the tinfoil packet on the barbecue and just heat through.

- Drizzle with some garlic oil and honey and finish with lemon zest and some black pepper. Place the claws at the side and serve with a simple salad.

Ingredients

2 Irish lobsters

50ml olive oil infused with roasted garlic oil (see page 56)

Local honey, olive oil, lemon zest, sea salt, black pepper

Smoked salmon

with boxty potato cake, horseradish mayonnaise and watercress

Ingredients

24 slices of smoked salmon

Potato cakes

300g mashed potato

300g grated raw potato

300g flour

1 egg

100ml buttermilk

zest of 1 lemon

100ml lemon and horseradish mayonnaise (see page 85)

watercress

David Brown is one of our favourite fish suppliers. He is a local man who runs a great seafood shop just outside the nearby town of Youghal where he also sells smoked salmon produced to a recipe that was developed years ago by his father. It's a fine example of a great local business based on traditional skills and ethics.

The fish are sourced from farms in Irish waters off the west coast and the smoke comes from oak sawdust. The salmon are exposed to anything up to 12 hours cold smoke.
It all depends on the size of the fish, the amount of salting and even the weather. The skill of the smoker means that each fish will end up with the same texture and the same gentle, but very distinctive, smoky flavour.

In this dish, we slice the smoked salmon differently from the usual way. In other words, instead of cutting thin slices along the fish, with the grain so to speak, here we cut thin slices right through the fish in sections or "silhouettes". This means that each slice has within it all the elements of the fish.

Throughout the year we like to serve smoked salmon with a range of garnishes.

Horseradish and lemon juice are, of course, very classical but it's worth ringing the changes with elements like beetroot, orange and *fromage frais*. One of my own favourite accompaniments is freshly made potato cakes.

- Combine the mash with the grated potato in a mixing bowl.

- Add the egg, buttermilk and the lemon zest. Mix well.

- Beat in the flour and season to taste.

- Shape into 8 equal balls and then press them into flat cakes.

- Cook the potato cakes on a low heat in a non-stick pan until brown and crisp.

- Divide the smoked salmon between 4 plates.

- Serve with potato cakes, horseradish mayonnaise, lemon zest and a little watercress.

Organic salmon and radish

Ingredients

500g organic salmon,
sliced in tranches

zest of 1 lemon

olive oil, black pepper, sea salt

20 ultra-fresh radishes

This dish is very straightforward but there's a slight catch. You need the freshest radishes that you can lay your hands on. For that, you will need your own little garden. And, of course, you must have good organic salmon or wild salmon.

The radishes need to be pulled, washed and served all within the hour. This may sound a little bit extreme but it's true. As soon as you take those radishes from the ground, the flavour starts to fade.

In Ireland, since the ban on drift-net fishing, wild salmon is not just a great luxury. It's almost impossible to find because the anglers want the fish for themselves. But there is an alternative. The farmed organic salmon from Clare Island is a very high quality fish that is produced in an environmentally-friendly and sustainable way. The flesh is firm, tasty and has a great colour.

At The Cliff House this salmon is always featured on one of the menus. People seem to love salmon, just like they love chicken, even if they don't always look for quality.

This dish makes a great summer lunch or an easy starter.

- Pre-heat the oven to 120ºC.

- On 4 small oven-proof plates spread a little olive oil seasoned with the zest of the lemon. Sprinkle over some lemon zest, salt and pepper.

- Divide the tranches between the plates.

- Brush the salmon with olive oil and sprinkle with lemon zest, salt and pepper.

- Put in the oven for 10 minutes.

- Then finish by shaving the radishes very thinly over each plate.

Organic salmon

cucumber, herb cream and salmon caviar

We blow fresh, fragrant smoke under a glass dome below which sits the salmon. This gentle infusion of smoke gives the fish a little lift.

Salmon

- Season the sides of salmon with the watercress, orange salt, black pepper and the lemon zest.

- Fold the two sides together, cut in half and wrap it very tight in clingfilm. The best way to do this is by putting 3 layers of clingfilm on the work surface. Roll the salmon in it, then tie both ends.

- Bring a pot of water (that will fit the salmon rolls) to a gentle boil.

- Put salmon in the water and lower the temperature to the lowest possible.

- The salmon needs to cook for 5 minutes; then turn off the heat and let it cool in the water. When it has completely cooled, remove from the water and leave in the fridge for at least 4 hours.

Cucumber

- Peel one of the cucumbers and dice it into very small cubes; marinate with vinegar, sugar, salt and pepper, then add fresh horseradish to taste and the zest of ½ lemon.

- Juice the other cucumber with the skin on and season to taste. For every 100ml of juice use one leaf of gelatine to set it; soak gelatine in cold water for 5 minutes, then heat half of the juice and dissolve the gelatine in it, mix with the rest of the juice and pour it in a suitable container. Leave in the fridge to set.

Herb cream

- Season and whip the cream until fluffy. Fold in the mixed herbs with the lemon zest. Then let it set in a food container in the fridge.

Remove the fish from the fridge, and remove the clingfilm. Carefully slice nice steaks of the salmon and arrange them in the middle of the plates. Sprinkle with orange salt and pepper.

On either side, arrange the sweet and sour cucumber and scoop some herb cream on top. On top of the cream place some salmon eggs.

Slice the cucumber jelly into cubes and arrange on the other two sides. If you wish, try to catch some smoke under a glass dome and place on top of the dish. When presenting, lift the dome for a dramatic effect.

Ingredients

Ballotine of salmon
1 organic salmon ⅔ size
(filleted, de-boned, 2 sides, skin on)

1 tbsp watercress, chopped

zest of 1 lemon, black pepper

orange sea salt (100g coarse sea salt infused with the zest of 2 oranges and the juice of one)

clingfilm

Cucumber
2 cucumbers

gelatine leaves (1 leaf to every 100ml cucumber juice)

80ml white wine vinegar

20g sugar

lemon zest and grated horseradish

salt and black pepper

Herb cream
150ml cream

2 tbsp mixed chopped herbs (chervil, parsley, tarragon, dill)

zest of ½ lemon, pepper and salt

Salmon caviar
50g Keta salmon eggs

Scallops and green asparagus

Ingredients

20 West Cork scallops

24 green asparagus spears

agar agar

2g soy lecithin (from the pharmacy or wholefood shop)

zest of 1 lemon

It's weird but true. You can't get scallops in the shell in Ireland.

Most wild scallops are harvested by simply scraping the sea bed but this method is very destructive of the ocean floor. The sustainable alternative is scallops harvested by divers, which not only is greener and more ecologically sound, but it delivers better quality too.
You have to pay the price for all that extra labour.

At The Cliff House, I insist on diver scallops.
I serve them with green asparagus and a sauce made from the roe. The asparagus is prepared in several different ways in order to give the dish structure and depth.

- Cut off the top 4cm of the asparagus tips. Juice the stalks and measure the amount. Season.

- To every 100ml of juice add 1g agar agar. Bring to the boil.

- Simmer for 2 minutes and then pour into a flat tray. Set aside in the fridge.

- Take 4 asparagus tips, halve them lengthways and make a batter of flour and beer (see page 57).

- Remove the roe of the scallops and place in a small saucepan, just covered with water.

- Bring to a soft boil and simmer for 10 minutes.

- Strain and season. Discard the roe.

- With a hand-held blender dissolve the lecithin in the roe water at a rate of 2g per 400ml. Let it foam up.

- Blanch the remaining asparagus tips, drain, and cover with olive oil, pepper and salt and add lemon zest.

- Fry the scallops in a non-stick pan until crisp on both sides.

- Deep-fry the tips in the batter until crisp and golden.

- Foam up the roe water and lecithin mixture once more.

- Slice the asparagus "jelly" in thin strips and place on the plate.

- Put the asparagus tips in the centre of the plate.

- Arrange the scallops on the plate and scoop the foam over them.

- Lastly, add the crisp asparagus fritters.

Hake with cherries

yoghurt, wild fennel and soda bread

Ingredients

4 x 90g hake fillets, skin on

100g fresh cherries, stoned

100ml organic yoghurt

2 slices soda bread

20g pistachio nuts

20g dried organic yoghurt

1 lemon

fresh wild fennel leaves and flowers

seasoning, pistachio oil

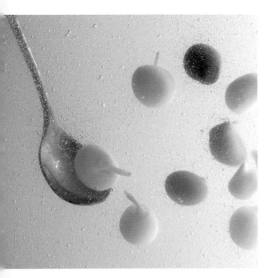

This dish is very much in tune with the season in which it was dreamed up. It was the very end of June, the first cherries had just arrived in the kitchen and hake was at its very best.

Fish and fruit? It may sound weird but there are lots of precedents. Think of sole veronique with grapes and sole Picasso which is almost a warm fish and fruit salad. Both are dishes from the good old days, so it's not so daring.

The thing about the first of the cherries is that they are not very ripe. In fact, beyond the natural tartness of the fruit acids, there is a savoury kind of quality. The yoghurt adds both richness and a tangy kick at the same time. The crunch comes from the soda bread, pistachios and lemon zest.

It's almost as good made with cod if hake happens to be unavailable.

- Crumble the soda bread and dry in a medium oven.

- Roast the pistachio nuts in a dry pan.

- Season the yoghurt with black pepper and lemon zest.

- Fry the hake fillets, skin side down until the meat starts to go opaque.

- Then turn over.

- When the hake is almost cooked, remove from the pan.

- Keep in a warm place.

- Fry the cherries in the same pan as the hake, tossing them until they caramelise.

- Add lemon juice and a teaspoon of pistachio oil and season.

- Place the hake on the plate and remove the skin.

- Sprinkle on the crisp soda bread, dried yoghurt and zest of the lemon.

- Spoon a little yoghurt on the side.

- Surround with the cherries and dress with the flowers and wild fennel leaves.

Roasted hake with barley "risotto"

rocket leaves and cheddar

Ingredients

4 x 200g hake fillets, skin on

100ml cider

zest of 1 lemon, sea salt,
black pepper, olive oil

150g barley

600ml vegetable stock (see page 228)

1 shallot, very finely diced

1 clove garlic, crushed

1 tsp thyme, chopped

50g mature Irish Cheddar, grated
(and some extra for serving)

40ml olive oil

1 bunch flatleaf parsley, finely chopped

½ bunch rocket leaves

Hake is one of the great fish but for some reason it's not very popular in Holland. So when I came to Ireland it was something with which I was not really familiar. I soon discovered how versatile and flavourful it is and was instantly converted. The Irish and the Spanish are the world's great hake enthusiasts.

Barley is much more Irish than rice and, anyway, it makes a great risotto. Okay, not an official risotto, but it's barley given the risotto treatment. This is a dish with a heart and a soul and fish works amazingly well with the...er... barley!

- Pre-heat the oven to 200°C.

- Marinate the hake fillets with some olive oil, zest of lemon, pepper and salt.

- Place them in an oven-proof dish and pour over the cider.

- Place in the oven for 15 minutes.

- Put 2 tbsp olive oil into a medium-sized pan and add the shallots, garlic and thyme.

- Warm through and add the barley.

- Add a quarter of the vegetable stock and stir until absorbed.

- Continue adding the stock until it has been absorbed and the barley is cooked.

- Set aside and check the fish.

- Finish the barley by adding the rest of the olive oil and the grated cheese.

- Add the parsley and season to taste.

- Serve the hake on a bed of risotto on large plates.

- The cooking juices can be mixed with some olive oil and drizzled around the dish.

- Dress the hake with some cheddar shavings and rocket.

Poached cod, sea vegetables

leeks, bacon and egg yolk with fennel infusion

My wife Wendy is a great cook and she loves to eat fish.

When I see what she can produce under pressure – two young boys who look like their father, very difficult - I realise that most professional chefs could learn a thing or two from her.

I know that I am very lucky to have Wendy as my partner.

- Pre-heat the oven to 170°C.
- Marinate the cod fillets in the Pernod, oil and lemon zest.
- Fry the leek pieces in a non-stick pan and place on an oven tray.
- Add a dash of water, thyme springs and a knob of butter.
- Cover with foil and put in the oven for 35 minutes.
- Juice the fennel and the carrot; add gelatine to juices.
- Bring to the boil and add a 1 tsp of oil.
- Reduce until it thickens and add 1 tbsp of Pernod.
- Set aside.

- Heat the fish stock and add the sea vegetables. Simmer for 1 minute. Strain and put the sea vegetables aside.
- Whizz the liquid with a hand blender.
- Season to taste and add the lemon oil.
- Gently poach the cod fillets in this mixture until the fish is just done and almost falls apart.
- Remove and put on a tray.
- Strain the cooking liquid into a pot and use it to poach 4 egg yolks
- Roughly chop the sea vegetables and spread on top of the cod.
- Arrange on plates with a piece of leek beside each fillet and a poached egg yolk on top of each leek.
- Fill a syringe with the infusion and inject into the centre of the cod.
- Place some crispy leeks on top of the cod together with some crispy bacon and mizuna leaves.
- Serve immediately.

Ingredients

Cod
4 x 100g cod fillets

1 tbsp Pernod

1 tbsp grapeseed oil

zest of ½ a lemon

Leek
4 x 3cm slices of leek

2 thyme sprigs

butter

Fennel infusion
2 fennel bulbs

1 carrot

1 leaf of gelatine

Pernod, olive oil, sea salt

Sea vegetables
30g sea vegetables

200ml fish stock

30ml lemon oil

Garnish
crispy leek pieces

crispy bacon

mizuna greens

4 egg yolks

Monkfish with smoke

potato, broad beans and oregano

Ingredients

4 monkfish fillets, 180g each

4 large potatoes

20g prawn dust (tail and head shells dried in a dehydrator or a very cool oven and ground in a coffee grinder)

olive oil, lemon zest, sea vegetables, salt and black pepper

Foam

200ml potato cooking water

1.8g soy lecithin

zest of ½ lemon

oregano leaves

10ml olive oil

seasoning

Garnish

broad beans, podded, skinned and blanched

black potato galettes: potato purée with squid ink, dried to make small discs

potato cubes, blanched in salted water

borage flowers and oregano

This is a dish that was created during the summer and it was a big success both as a starter and a main course.

The monkfish is wrapped in spaghetti of potato, and then cooked until crisp in a pan, the potato adding a texture and depth of flavour that really suits the fish. It will seal in all the juices and the end result will be worth all the effort.

As a sauce we use the water in which the potato cubes are cooked, add seasoning and aerate it with soy lecithin. This is actually an egg substitute and can create a foam as light as air, but full of the original, natural flavour.

The smoke creates an extra dimension and is a Cliff House Hotel special effect that seems to impress people every time.

- Pre-heat the oven to 170°C.

- Marinate the monkfish fillets with a splash of olive oil, lemon zest, salt, prawn dust and pepper.

- Make spaghetti of the potatoes (using a Japanese vegetable turner).

- Wrap the monkfish fillets in a thin layer of potato spaghetti.

- In a non-stick frying pan heat some oil and cook the monkfish until golden brown on all sides. Add the potato cubes.

- Then put in the oven for 8 minutes.

- Heat the potato water and add the oregano, lemon zest, olive oil, and season.

- Then add the lecithin and mix thoroughly with a hand blender.

- Strain, and taste.

- Foam up, using a spoon behind the turning area of the blender to create maximum turbulence.

- Heat the broad beans in some of the potato water and season.

- To serve cut the monkfish in medallions and arrange the broad beans and potato cubes around them.

- Skim the frothy foam and spoon on and around the monkfish.

- Garnish with borage flowers and oregano and serve directly.

- If you wish, try to catch some smoke under a glass dome and put on top of the dish.

- When presenting, lift the dome for a dramatic effect.

Oven-roasted sea bass

Ingredients

4 whole sea bass, each weighing
500-600g (scaled and gutted)

rosemary

thyme

2 fennel bulbs, quartered

2 lemons, quartered

4 garlic cloves

olive oil, black pepper, sea salt

This is a very straightforward dish and quite easy to prepare. The only thing that you could possibly find daunting about it is the fact that it involves whole fish and, of course, whole fish involve bones. But it is very striking and quite dramatic.

In Ireland there are strict regulations when it comes to wild sea bass and this is in order to preserve the species. Because there are very severe limits on how and when sea bass can be caught it is a rare pleasure and all the more enjoyable for that.

I love wild seabass and I was very tempted to buy them from the anglers who bring them to the door. But I soon found that I would be breaking the law. So I have to get my wild sea bass from France, where the regulations are a lot less strict.

You can, of course, use the farmed fish. It's quite a good alternative especially these days as fish farms are getting better and better and standards are being raised all the time.

Serve this dish with mixed leaves and a potato salad.

- Pre-heat the oven to 200°C.

- Rub the sea bass all over with olive oil, salt and pepper.

- Crush the garlic and rub into the cavity.

- Put sprigs of rosemary and thyme in the cavity.

- Do the same with the lemon and the fennel (2 quarters per fish).

- Put in the oven and roast the fish until cooked – this will take about 25 minutes.

- Serve on a big plate.

Joy and peace

Believe me, it's not romantic. Yes, it's satisfying.
Yes, there's a buzz but it's not romantic.

I didn't know that when I was sixteen and I delivered 33 hand-written letters, personally, to the best restaurants in Amsterdam. But after a year in the kitchen at the local hotel with all those pork chops, I knew two things. I knew I wanted to be a chef and I knew I wanted to move on. Even just by the two-and-a-half hour train journey from Groningen to Amsterdam.

I got a great training under Wynand Vogel at Les Quatre Canetons in Amsterdam and after a year applied for a job at The Vermeer restaurant in Amsterdam, which was under Gert Jan Hageman and known as the most progressive kitchen in Holland. It had just got a Michelin star, but also had a reputation for having the friendliest kitchen in the business. Gert Jan had a way of working that was very liberal and open, based on trust. Just before I started my stint with his team, he suddenly moved to Restaurant Hotel Vreugd & Rust to replace Henk Savelberg.

Gert Jan called me and said that he was moving on, and if I was interested, I could go with him. If I did not, he understood and my position at The Vermeer was still secure. I decided to go with him.

There was a big difference. The dishes, the mentality, the team, even the smell of the kitchen was different.

Gert Jan was something of a creative rebel. He even had a barbecue in the kitchen, worked with lots of different spices and used countless influences from his culinary travels.

This was it, I thought. The kitchen started work at 11 am and first there was coffee and a discussion. Everything was relaxed while organised, but there was something wrong: the buzz and excitement that he had stirred up in Amsterdam was not there, his style of cooking did not get the same response. Why? Because this area of the country was very conservative and the people were used to the Henk Savelberg way of cooking.

Shortly after my seven-month adventure with Gert Jan started, Savelberg returned to his beloved Vreugd & Rust. It was awful to see the team start to fall apart, insecurity creeping in and people fearing for their jobs. Savelberg returned with a full brigade but I was fortunate to be one of only two to survive the change. Fortunate in that I was given the chance to stay and work with his team.

Vreugd en Rust means "Joy and Peace". Whatever about the joy, there was precious little peace in the job, probably because this was the number one restaurant in Holland at the time.

The style of Henk Savelberg was deeply traditional and French but with a modern Dutch twist. There were twenty chefs in the kitchen and everything was done with true military precision. It was the opposite of the Gert Jan kitchen.

They told me that we started at nine o'clock. So I turned up for my first day's work at five to nine and everyone else was already there working. That was the kind of place it was. You gave even more than was expected of you. You worked very, very hard because Savelberg was a brilliant and very modest guy who simply knew what worked and, more importantly, how to make us want to make it work.

One day a chef gave me a copy of *White Heat* by Marco Pierre White. And if I had never been given the book, maybe I would never have ended up working in Britain.

Paranoia and testosterone:

how not to do it

I'm never very happy when chefs start to name-check other chefs. "I worked with so-and-so" ends up sounding like "I helped to create so-and-so." But the path that you take through the restaurant business and the people you meet along the way leave some kind of mark, either positive or negative. I mean you can end up not doing something or other because your one-time boss, now famous, did it that way.

The best chef I ever worked for was Henk Savelberg in The Hague but young chefs don't stay in one place for very long. As always happens, even in the best kitchens, one of my workmates got itchy feet and left Holland to go travelling.

He didn't get very far and ended up running a Pierre Victoire restaurant (one of a franchised chain of French bistros) in one of Scotland's not-so-glamorous towns, Dundee. This was at a time when the Pierre Victoire concept was still about cooking from scratch rather than getting all the dishes supplied from a central kitchen and just finishing them in the kitchen.

Maybe the owners of the chain realised something important. I went over to Scotland to give a hand and we had fun but cooking from scratch and trying to meet the really low price points that were Pierre Victoire's main attraction was too much. The business folded

after only four months. Maybe Dundee just wasn't ready for a bargain bistro.

But while I was there I got to eat in David Wilson's famous Peat Inn near St Andrew's in Fife which he had opened way back in 1972 and which had earned him Scotland's first Michelin star. Wilson was a big champion of local produce and his menus were always about the best seasonal raw materials, something that is much more common now than it was back in the 1990s.

Working in Dundee was fun but it was really a diversion. I knew I needed to get back into the business, the serious end of the restaurant business and so I ended up heading south to Shinwell in Berkshire where the young John Burton-Race took me on at L'Ortolan, the restaurant that he put well and truly on the map before heading off to the Landmark Hotel and a pretty chaotic later career. Mind you, I only spent a fortnight working for him.

Despite my short stay, I could see that he was obsessional and made a virtue of paranoia, telling us that "only the paranoid survive." He was difficult, to say the least, but he was a great chef and he had a very loyal following. I knew when I went there that it was not going to be a walk in the park but I had to ask myself if all of the angst and the general warfare in

I knew I needed to get back into the business,
the serious end of the restaurant business.

Paranoia and testosterone:
how not to do it

He was old-fashioned in ways, particularly in how he dealt
with us minions and underlings.

the kitchen was worth it and, of course, the answer was no. And so I went to London and managed to get a job with Pierre Koffmann at La Tante Claire in Chelsea (in what is now Restaurant Gordon Ramsay). Koffmann had started cooking in England with Michel Roux at the Waterside Inn, not a million miles from the site of L'Ortolan. He opened La Tante Claire way back in 1977 where his signature dish of pig's trotter stuffed with truffles became the talk of London.

He was old-fashioned in ways, particularly in how he dealt with us minions and underlings. He never, ever spoke to us. Instructions and, I guess, edicts, were issued through a sous-chef. He was very formal and very imposing, a tall figure in his impeccable whites.

He had never met a chef taller than himself until he met me. But I learned a lot from him, even if it was indirectly.

When Marco Pierre White left Le Gavroche (where Albert Roux called him, amazingly, "my little lamb"), he joined the kitchen at La Tante Claire where Koffmann may or may not have spoken to him. In any event, he moved on to work with Raymond Blanc at Le Manoir aux Quat' Saisons and later with Nico Ladenis at Ninety Park Lane before opening Harvey's on Wandsworth Common where Bruce Poole now

has Chez Bruce. He was awarded a Michelin star within months of opening in 1987 and a second one followed in 1988.

After six months at La Tante Claire, I got a job with Marco Pierre White who by this stage had left Wandsworth for the much posher Hyde Park Hotel in Kensington. He was also working on Canteen in Chelsea Harbour and The Criterion in Piccadilly at this stage.

The kitchen was a tough, loud environment. There was a lot of testosterone. And in this environment teamwork is bound to suffer because everyone wants to impress the boss.

But it was an interesting experience. The produce was fantastic, simply the best. Every-thing, in a sense, was possible, there were no limits, the budget would always stretch. And so I learned some great dishes but I knew that it was not for me.

It was all a bit patronising and sometimes it felt like you were being treated like a little kid. Some people thrive in that kind of environment, and if you want to take a holiday from thinking for yourself it's fine, but it didn't really suit me. All in all, it was a pretty mixed experience but I have to say that I benefitted in one strange way: I learned how not to run a restaurant.

And I learned how much insecurity there can be in the upper echelons of the cheffing world. In London at that time a lot of the big names were constantly watching each other, copying each other, usually with a little twist for originality, sometimes acknowledging the debt like Marco Pierre White's pig's trotter which was really Pierre Koffmann's pig's trotter but which was flagged as being "in honour of Pierre Koffmann."

I know this sounds a bit crazy, but cooking in restaurants at that level where there is so much money and all sorts of luxury ingredients, is very limiting. It has to be expensive.

It was a big relief in many ways to come back to Les Quatres Canetons in Amsterdam as head chef. But the big change came when I went to a restaurant that dared to re-write the rules, that didn't shy away from simplicity, but made a virtue of it instead.

And it was in a greenhouse.

Warm sauces

Now, I have to admit that I have a real fetish about this one and I only eat it at home because I think I am the only one who can make it perfectly.

Hollandaise sauce

Hollandaise sauce is perhaps the best known and loved of the classic French sauces. It is seen as difficult but just requires some attention and care to make it work.

The only things you need are a pot with boiling water, suitable mixing bowl, whisk and the simple ingredients. In the traditional cookbooks clarified butter is specified to make this sauce but ordinary butter will do fine. You will need 2 eggs, white wine vinegar, water, and 200g butter.

- Separate the eggs and keep the whites to make meringue.
- Measure the vinegar by filling half an eggshell with it. You will need four half eggshellfuls.
- Do the same with water - two half eggshellfuls.
- Melt the butter and keep warm.
- Whisk the egg, water and vinegar mixture with a pinch of salt.
- Put on top of the boiling water and whisk until the mixture is fluffy and starts bubbling.

- Then take the boiling water off the heat and, drop by drop, add the melted butter, whisking all the time.
- Return to the heat and keep stirring for 1 minute. Season to taste.
- If you are not going to use the sauce right away, just add a drop of cream and keep in a warm place.

Sauce mousseline

100ml whipped cream

- Add the whipped cream to the hollandaise and fold it in- serve directly.

Sauce maltaise

Add the zest and the juice of 1 orange to the hollandaise and serve with poached fish.

Sauce supreme

This is a classic created by the great French chef Antoine Careme. You just take your basic hollandaise and add 2 tbsp veal jus and 2 tbsp poultry jus and mix thoroughly.

Such sauces will never fail to give genuine pleasure but sometimes we tend to forget about them. Good taste and wonderful flavours never really go out of fashion.

As a commis chef I had to learn how to make all the variations on the hollandaise theme and one of my favourites was the béarnaise. Now, I have to admit that I have a real fetish about this one and I only eat it at home because I think I am the only one who can make it perfectly according to my rules. I have been disappointed by béarnaise sauce just too often when eating out in restaurants.

Now, I have to stress that this is not the reason for the absence of béarnaise sauce from the menu at The Cliff House. No, the reason is this. It's just too French and The Cliff House is an Irish restaurant.

Why does everything have to come from the French classical tradition?

But, I have to admit that this sauce has a special place in my life. And there is nothing better with grilled beef and fries. I just keep it for home. Here goes...

Béarnaise Sauce

1 tbsp shallots, chopped
1 tbsp chervil, chopped
1 tbsp tarragon, chopped
1 sprig of thyme
¼ bay leaf
100ml white wine
100ml white wine vinegar
8 peppercorns, crushed

Put these ingredients into a small pot and bring to the boil. Reduce the mixture to about one quarter of the original volume and strain.

- Cut 175g of butter into small cubes.
- Take 2 egg yolks and add to the reduced liquid.
- Whisk on a gentle heat until it gets fluffy and as thick as custard.
- Then add the cubes of butter, just a few at a time, and keep whisking until smooth.
- Season to taste and finish by adding 2 tbsp chopped chervil and tarragon.
- Serve directly.

Beurre blanc
(classic white butter sauce)

The words "beurre blanc" (literally "white butter") appear on almost every restaurant menu, usually with fish or asparagus. And almost invariably it is made with cream which means that it's an impostor. There's no cream in a true beurre blanc. To be precise (and chefs have to be precise and accurate), a beurre blanc made with cream is a beurre nantais but I suppose it doesn't sound as good. Or at least it doesn't sound comfortably familiar.

Again with this type of sauce you can add anything you like, from rosemary to chives, from vanilla to saffron. This sauce can adapt to almost every added flavor and this is what makes it so popular with chefs.

I will tell you how to make both versions, beurre blanc and beurre nantais.

Beurre blanc

2 shallots, sliced into rings
125ml white wine vinegar
125ml fish stock (see page 232)
¼ bay leaf
4 peppercorns, crushed
150g butter (in small cubes)

- Place all ingredients except the butter in a pot and bring to the boil.
- Reduce to ⅓ of the original amount.
- Remove from the heat and strain.
- Return the strained liquid to the pot.
- Whisk the butter into the base mixture, one quarter at a time.
- Season to taste.
- Serve directly.

For the beurre nantais, add 100ml of cream at the start.

Warm sauces

Base sauce

This sauce is the most common in the professional kitchen and it is easier than you think. You just need a good base of veal, lamb or beef stock. That is the heart and soul of a good sauce. Chicken stock is not suitable as it becomes very bitter and harsh as it is reduced.

As the stock reduces it will get concentrated and the flavour will increase significantly and it will also become thicker in a natural way. This is thanks to the collagen, a gelatinous substance, which is found in the bones.

The more you reduce a sauce the higher the concentration of this will become and the thicker the sauce. But do remember that if you overcook or over-reduce any stock it will become bitter and very sticky. Once you reach this stage there is no going back. People sometimes try adding water but the damage has been done and it won't be good to eat.

2 ltr base stock (beef, lamb or veal)
300ml red wine
2 shallots, sliced into rings
1 garlic clove, crushed
2 sprigs of thyme
½ bay leaf
1 tbsp neutral oil, such as grapeseed

- Put the shallots, garlic, thyme and bay leaf in a pot with oil and bring to the boil.
- Cook until the shallots caramelise.
- Add the red wine and reduce until it becomes syrupy.
- Add 2 ladles of stock and let it reduce to ⅓ of the amount.
- Repeat until all the stock has been used.
- At this point, the liquid will have thickened and started to shine.
- Strain through a fine sieve.
- Serve right away or cool it and put in the fridge.

Warm sauces

The base sauce can be used to make several sauces such as:

Pepper sauce
200ml base sauce
2 tbsp black peppercorns, ground or crushed

- Dry roast the peppercorns for 1-2 minutes in a pot.
- Add the base sauce and bring to the boil.
- Season to taste and serve.

For a creamy sauce just replace 50ml of the base with cream.

You can also play with the pepper element by using pink or green peppercorns, but it is best to soak them in hot water before adding. This will soften them and release the flavour.

And there are lots of other possibilities. Use 200ml of the base sauce to make the following:

Mustard sauce: Add 2 tbsp grain mustard.

Horseradish sauce: Add 50g grated horseradish.

Murphy's sauce: Add 50ml Murphy's Stout and 1 tsp horseradish.

Roast garlic sauce: Add 50g puréed roast garlic and 1 tsp chopped thyme.

Mint sauce: Add 2 tbsp finely sliced mint leaves and 1 tbsp mint jelly.

Blueberry sauce: Add 50g blueberries and 1 tbsp blackcurrant syrup.

Butter sauce: Add 50g butter.

Cream sauce: Add 100ml whipped cream and 1 tbsp chopped parsley to 150ml base sauce.

Grazing – the kindest cuts

Fashion is a strange thing. Sometimes you can understand how something got to be popular. Like fish and chips. Or *The Simpsons*. But at other times, it's hard to follow.

Take meat, for example. The most fashionable cuts of meat are nice to eat. But the less fashionable cuts have more flavour. Okay, most of them take a bit longer to cook, to break down the tougher fibres, but they just have more taste.

Which would you rather eat, for sheer flavour, a fillet steak that melts on your tongue or a skirt steak that has to be cut thinly across the fibres to make it chewable? That tough old flank steak (we call it the piano piece in Holland) will deliver mountains more taste. And that's the main reason (the other one is cheapness) that French bistros choose it for steak and frites.

Beef is fantastic in Ireland, probably because it's grass-fed. When we complain about the climate here we should remember that without it we would not have the best beef in the world. But fillet is not the best bit of beef and, unfortunately in a way, this is a fillet of beef kind of restaurant.

I tried serving slowly braised beef cheeks but our customers were not even tempted. They wanted fillet rather than flavour.

And, of course, in this business, the customer is always right, even when he's wrong.

Maybe beef cheeks are the most unfashionable cut of beef but perhaps they are beaten by marrow bones. I know it's not exactly a cut of meat but it has the greatest flavour of all, a kind of intensity that sticks to your palate. I like to cook marrow bones with snails. In fact, I call the dish "lost snails", but that's another story.

Ever since my umami moment with oxtail soup when I was five or six, I've been a lover of beef. For me, one of the best cuts is a rib-eye steak done very carefully on the barbecue. You can't have it rare because the connective tissues need just enough heat to melt, so the perfect rib-eye is always medium but still really juicy. And don't be tempted to cut off the fat. There's a lot of flavour in it. If you don't believe me just remember this: the best chips in the world are fried in beef dripping. So, render the fat and brush the meat with it as it cooks.

The best thing with a rib-eye steak is a good béarnaise sauce made using your own homemade tarragon vinegar flavoured with the herb stalks and some white peppercorns and unsalted butter so you can control the seasoning.

Beef has to be hung but most people are lucky to buy beef that has been aged more than a week. A fortnight is average in a good butcher's and you will get 28 days maximum if you look very hard. I like my beef aged a bit more: 36 to 38 days is ideal and I have to do this myself.

The ageing means that the meat's natural enzymes get to break down the fibres and make them edible. As the enzymes get to work and the meat relaxes, the true flavour of the meat is liberated. Sometimes people think that ageing puts flavour into the meat but it actually lets it out, frees it from captivity.

The main reason why well-aged meat is so hard to come by is that ageing involves a loss of moisture and this translates into a loss of weight. So the butcher is selling you something that has shrunk a lot since the animal was slaughtered. Intelligent people understand this and are happy to pay more for meat that has been hung for several weeks, so as to compensate the butcher both for the loss of weight and for the time involved. But you can see why meat is not given much ageing as a rule. It's like most businesses: people who sell meat want to get a turnaround as quickly as is practical.

Grazing – the kindest cuts

The most fashionable cuts of meat are nice to eat.
But the less fashionable cuts have more flavour.

Coming back to fashion, what about goat? Goat doesn't have a fashionable cut, at least not in this part of the world. Goat is unfashionable from the top of its horns to the tip of its tail. But it sure tastes good.

I marinated and cured some wild Irish mountain goat and it was superb. But it's hard to sell on a menu. The trick is to partner it with something really luxurious like foie gras. Then the average customer feels okay about ordering it. And it happens to be a very good combination anyway.

One of the great things about The Cliff House is that it's a small hotel and guests are always comparing notes. This means that if you have a couple of adventurous palates staying and they try something like goat, the word will spread that it's good.

It worked for crubeens. I had read about them, of course. They are still sold in a big way in Cork and people swear that they are just the thing after you have drunk a lot of stout. I just had to try cooking them myself.

Crubeens, or pig's trotters, are not exactly fashionable but it's amazing how often they feature, in one form or another, on very fashionable menus. I suppose it's because chefs love the flavour and the textures involved and they like to play with them.

I vacuum-pack crubeens with sage and apple and cook them for 24 hours at 62°C. After that, they are literally like jelly and I just slice them thinly and serve them with parsley soup. They also go brilliantly with beetroot and grainy mustard.

Nature is good. If the cheaper cuts didn't taste so good, where would we be? I mean, rack of lamb and leg of lamb are lovely but how many do you get off one animal? There's all the other stuff left and with careful cooking it can surpass the more expensive, more fashionable bits.

I reckon that almost all good chefs have a kind of thrifty streak. And because we spend so long in the kitchen we don't mind if something takes ages to cook. The average person, who spends so much time commuting, is a bit turned off by the idea of leaving a piece of meat to simmer for hours. But this is really shortsighted. What could be better than coming home to, say, tender lamb shanks that have been in a very low oven since breakfast time, or even since the night before? Long, slow cooking releases flavours and even textures that you never guessed were there.

One of the cuts with the best flavour that I've cooked since I moved to Ireland was rump of lamb which I got from Michael McGrath in Lismore. I minced the fat, rendered it and then cooked the rump in its own fat at a low temperature for hours and hours. And then I finished it on the barbecue. The unexpected combination of these two very different cooking techniques produced a taste that was really sensational.

Michael McGrath's lamb is very unusual. People are always going on about traceability but Michael goes beyond that. He's a farmer and a butcher so he raises the lamb, kills it and butchers it. This is really very rare and I'm conscious that what I say about lamb here in these pages is based on his very particular lamb.

Irish lamb in general is very good and a lot of it is aged for about a fortnight. In Holland it doesn't seem to be aged at all.

Meat, poultry and game

Skeaghanore duck

with onions five ways and sweet potato tart

Ingredients

4 duck breasts trimmed,
but with their skin and fat

1 garlic clove

thyme salt

Szechuan pepper

4 small onions

1 red onion

2 white onions

1 sweet onion

500ml vegetable stock

bay leaf, thyme, butter

2 sweet potatoes

4 rounds of puff pastry

organic honey

100ml duck jus

It was thanks to the Midleton Farmers' Market that we discovered the ducks from Skeaghanore and it really was a discovery worth making. Eugene and Helena Hickey farm 120 acres of West Cork and until a few years ago they were dedicated dairy farmers. When they decided to diversify into ducks they brought something new to the market.

We always buy the whole duck as we have a use for every scrap of it. The legs and the necks go for making rillettes, the wings are glazed and go to feed the hungry staff, the carcass is used for stock, the hearts and gizzards are slowly cooked in the fat of the duck, the livers make a parfait, and finally the breasts make a main course.

- Pre-heat the oven to 175°C.

- Clean and peel the onions.

- Melt a knob of butter in a small pot. Add the four small onions, a bay leaf and seasoning. Cover with vegetable stock; braise gently until cooked.

- Slice the sweet onion into small cubes and put them in a pot with a knob of butter. Add some thyme sprigs and half a clove of garlic; cook very gently to a compote.

- Slice the red onion very thinly and sprinkle with salt; dry in a very cool oven.

- Peel the sweet potatoes and slice each in two. Boil for 4 minutes in salted water. Then strain and marinate with pepper, salt and honey.

- Cover each potato half with a pastry round and bake until crisp.

- Heat a non-stick pan; salt the skin of the duck breasts; place them skin side down in the pan.

- Slowly cook the duck skin golden brown and crisp then turn over and place the duck in the oven for 12 minutes.

- Remove from the oven and let rest for 2 minutes in a warm place.

- Slice the white onions very thinly; flour half of these rings and deep-fry. The rest of these onion rings are served raw.

- Assemble the dish by placing the compote of onion on the plate and build this up with the slow-cooked small onions, the deep-fried onion rings, the raw onion and the dried onion; place the potato pastry side down on the plate, and slice the duck - either in half or in four or five equal slices.

- Serve with a dash of olive oil and the duck jus on the side. If you have them, use chive, leek or onion flowers as a garnish.

Duck confit with apple and sage

Shane is the true Irish influence that we need at the senior level in the kitchen. From the start, he took charge of the soda bread, thank heaven. Who am I, as a Dutchman, to pretend to be able to do better with this great Irish classic?

Fair play to him, we couldn't do what we do at The Cliff House without Shane.

This recipe for duck with a very Irish twist was devised by him. We use duck legs from Skeaghanore in West Cork.

To confit the duck legs

- Crush the garlic, roughly chop the rosemary, tear the bay leaf and mix with 1 tbsp of coarse sea salt.

- Rub the duck legs with this mixture and leave to marinate overnight in the fridge.

- Cover the legs with the sunflower oil. Bring to a soft boil.

- Simmer the duck legs on the lowest heat possible for at least 4-6 hours.

- Cool.

- When the duck legs reach room temperature they are ready to be processed.

To make the rillettes

- Dice the onions and soften them in the butter.

- Break up the duck legs into pieces and add to the pan.

- Peel, core and cut the apples in chunky cubes and add to the pan.

- Stir vigorously until all is combined.

- Add the mustard, vinegar, seasoning and sliced sage and cook for 5 minutes.

- Serve on a plate with pan-fried soda bread (see page 42). Alternatively, press it into a terrine shape and chill overnight.

Ingredients

6 duck legs

1 garlic clove

1 sprig rosemary

1 bay leaf

sunflower oil

sea salt

6 confit duck legs

3 onions

3 Granny Smith apples

100g butter

1 tbsp Dijon mustard

2 tbsp white wine vinegar

1 bunch of sage

Chicken and beer

Ingredients

1 organic chicken (1.5 kg)

1 can of your favourite beer (0.5 litres)

1 lemon

2 leeks, sliced in 2cm rings

2 carrots, sliced in 2cm rings

2 onions, diced

12 baby potatoes, washed and halved

1 chicken stock cube

sprig of thyme

bay leaf

1 tbsp rapeseed oil

salt and pepper

For a lot of restaurants, chicken is all about playing safe. The average chicken doesn't taste of very much (some don't taste of anything at all), so the kitchen can use this bland meat as a vehicle for actual flavours. And, of course, it sells. Commercially, you just can't go wrong with chicken. In terms of real food, however, chicken can be a minefield.

The only way for a restaurant like ours to go is to work with proper free-range, organic chickens that actually taste of real chicken (which can be a bit of shock to some people), chickens that have proper structure and texture. They are not full of water and they need delicate handling.

The chickens that arrive in our kitchen are always organically reared and always whole so the first job is to get them de-boned. We use everything. The staff eat well off the legs, the breasts go to the guests, the carcasses make stock and the wings are a great late night snack.

The French have their coq au vin. We think the Irish should have their own chicken and beer dish, something that can be enjoyed by all the family because the alcohol will have evaporated while it is cooking. What stays is flavour!

- Pre-heat the oven to 170°C.

- Pour half of the beer into a roasting dish.

- Add the vegetables, thyme, bay leaf and potatoes and mix.

- Season with pepper and salt.

- Crush the chicken stock cube and mix with a dash of beer, 1 tbsp rapeseed oil and the lemon juice.

- Rub the chicken all over with this paste.

- Put the half-full beer can in the centre of the roasting dish, and place the chicken over it in an upright position with the beer can inserted into the cavity.

- Cover the chicken with aluminium foil.

- Cook the chicken for about 1 hour and then remove the foil.

- Cook for a further 15 minutes or until the chicken is cooked.

- Place the whole dish on the table before carving and serving.

Organic chicken

aromatic butter with confit artichokes

Ingredients

4 organic or free-range chicken
breasts with skin and first bone

8 confit baby artichokes (see page 64)

90g breadcrumbs

80g tartare butter (see page 44)

8 scallions

1 tbsp butter

40ml dry cider

1 bay leaf

The secret to this dish is the very aromatic butter that is carefully placed under the skin. It's not just about flavour, of course, because this chicken dish is beautifully moist too.

- Pre-heat the oven to 175°C.

- Mix the breadcrumbs with the tartare butter and put in a piping bag with a round nozzle.

- Take the chicken breast and, with your finger, make a little space under the skin.

- Carefully pipe the butter under the skin until it fills up. Repeat for all the fillets.

- Ensure that the butter is evenly spread and refrigerate the fillets for 30 minutes.

- Sear the chicken, skin side down, on a non-stick pan until golden brown.

- Then put on an oven tray and roast for 15 minutes or until cooked through.

- In the meantime slice the artichokes in quarters and put in a saucepan.

- Add the cider, a bay leaf and a knob of butter and bring to a soft boil.

- Slice the scallions at an angle in 3cm lengths and add to the warm artichokes. Toss together.

- When the chicken is cooked, remove from oven and carve as you wish.

- Serve directly with the artichokes.

Ballynatray pigeon

cottiers' kale, beetroot textures with juniper ice cream

There's nothing quite so free range as game. And if you want natural food, organic food and seasonal food, game has a very special role to play. Actually, we tend to think of game as being something for the cooler months but, for example, you can get pigeon all year round.

Many people think of game as always having a really strong, gamey taste. But a young pheasant that has been hung for just a week can taste very much like guinea fowl. Venison (not the buck in the rutting season!) just tastes meaty rather than strong or gamey.

At The Cliff House we like to work with game on the menu and source it from the 800-acre Ballynatray estate, near Youghal, where head keeper John Dawson looks after this very beautiful piece of Ireland on the banks of the Blackwater.

- Warm the beetroot juice in a pan and add the pepper, juniper berries and bay leaf.

- Let it come to the boil and season with salt.

- Add the pigeon breasts.

- Make sure that the breasts are covered with the beet juice. Put the lid on.

- Bring to a quick boil and turn the heat off.

- Let it cool.

- Crush the juniper berries and mix all components for the ice cream.

- Put in a saucepan and bring to a soft boil.

- Turn down the heat and simmer for 10 minutes. Strain the mixture and put into an ice cream machine to churn.

- Slice the kale in the thinnest strips possible and marinate with bay leaf oil and lemon zest.

- Season to taste.

- Reheat the pigeon breasts for 2 minutes on low heat.

- Then carve them neatly in equal slices and place on a warm plate.

- Divide the kale over the pigeon and scoop the ice cream on top.

Ingredients

Pigeon

4 pigeon breasts

100ml beetroot juice

6 peppercorns, crushed

6 juniper berries, crushed

½ bay leaf

sea salt

Juniper ice cream

See page 178

Cottiers' kale

100g cottiers' kale

bay leaf oil

lemon zest, pepper, sea salt

Garnish

marinated beetroot slices
(boil, peel, marinate in bay leaf oil)

beetroot jelly
(made the same way as cucumber jelly, page 113)

dried cottiers' kale
American or land cress

Venison with celeriac rémoulade

and vanilla foam

Ingredients

4 x 180g venison fillet steaks

250g celeriac, peeled and grated into a fine julienne

3 tbsp tartare sauce (see page 82)

2 egg yolks

90ml apple juice

1 tsp vanilla essence

seasoning

cress

brown soda bread

I first met Gareth, fresh from the Australian outback, when we worked together at de Kas in Amsterdam a few years ago.

When I asked him to create a dish for this book, he suggested kangaroo as it's a favourite raw material from home. You can imagine how enthusiastic I was about this fresh, local Irish ingredient! In the end he agreed to use the venison from the Ballynatray estate. Doubtless it's not the same as he had in mind, but it tastes great.

This recipe produces rare venison. Feel free to cook it for longer if you want it well done.

- Squeeze the julienne of celeriac with your hands and press out the juice.

- Mix with the tartare sauce, season to taste and set aside.

- Heat the frying pan and season the steaks.

- Fry them on both sides for 4 minutes; then wrap them in foil and keep warm.

- Put the egg yolks, apple juice and vanilla essence in a saucepan.

- Whisk on a low heat until frothy.

- Put some celeriac in the middle of the plate.

- Now put the steak on the plate and spoon over some foam.

- Garnish it with cress and serve directly with slices of brown soda bread.

Black pudding croquettes

with gooseberries

Ingredients

Croquettes

80g flour

80g butter

400ml milk

1 small glass cider

250g local black pudding

chives, chopped

rocket

flour

eggs

breadcrumbs

Compote

200g gooseberries

35g sugar

Black pudding is not, in itself, unique to Ireland but there is a particular character to the Irish version and it is hugely popular, especially at breakfast. At The Cliff House, we get through a lot of it and not just for breakfast. I like to use it occasionally in fish or shellfish dishes.

Mikey is a great member of the team. Like virtually every Irishman I've encountered, he is very keen on deep-frying. He is the king of the fryer treats in our kitchen and is forever developing new and unusual ones. I always say that you can take the fryer out of the kitchen, but not out of the Irish chef.

One of Mikey's own inventions is black pudding croquettes with gooseberries. This is really good and it seems to have universal appeal. People who would never dream of eating black pudding get stuck right in.

The idea is really well thought through and just goes to show the kind of talent that Mikey has.

- Melt the butter and add the flour. Stir over a low heat for 2 minutes until the flour is cooked.

- Heat the milk. Add the cider to the flour and butter and then slowly add the milk, being careful not to allow any lumps to form.

- Dice the black pudding coarsely and stir in.

- Add the chives to the mixture and season to taste.

- Spread the mixture on a tray and refrigerate.

- When the mixture is cold, put it into a piping bag and pipe out in lines onto parchment.

- Cut into 6cm lengths. Dip them in flour, egg and finally breadcrumbs.

- Deep-fry until crisp and deep gold in colour.

- Garnish with a little rocket.

Compote

- Combine the gooseberries, sugar and a dash of water and cook on a low heat until the fruit becomes soft and syrupy. Serve with the croquettes.

Sausage rolls

After a busy service the boys have a really good appetite. So, what to eat?

The sausages are calling but we can go one better: real sausage rolls. And I mean real, proper, homemade.

The commercial version is disgusting, a soggy mixture of fat and flour. It has no place in a kitchen like ours, so we make our own. If you spend your day trying to produce great food, you want to end up eating something that may be simple but still really good.

You need only bread dough and minced meat. Nothing could be simpler. I often make these sausage rolls with my sons if we have a little celebration. And it's great fun.

- Preheat the oven to 175°C.

- Mix the flour with the salt and sugar in a bowl.

- Combine the egg with milk and dissolve the yeast in this mixture.

- Melt the butter and, using a hand-held blender, combine it with the milk mixture.

- Now make a dough by working the liquid mixture into the flour.

- Work the dough until it is elastic. It should not be sticky. If it is, just add some more flour.

- Cut the dough into sixteen equal pieces and work them into little rounds.

- Cover with a tea towel and leave to rise.

- Now put the mince, onion, garlic and seasoning in a mixing bowl.

- Mix well and then add the eggs and milk.

- Then add the breadcrumbs and combine until the mixture is fairly smooth.

- Put the mixture into a piping bag.

- Flour the work surface and dust the bread rounds with flour.

- Use a rolling pin to turn the bread rounds into thin ovals.

- Pipe the filling onto the dough and close up tightly.

- Put them, with the closed sides down, on a non-stick baking tray.

- Leave the sausage rolls to rise for 20 minutes.

- Brush the sausage rolls with egg wash and sprinkle with salt.

- Bake for 30 minutes until golden brown and serve with home-made tomato ketchup.

Ingredients

Bread dough

500g flour

10g sugar

10g salt

75g butter

1 egg

300ml warm milk

40g yeast

Stuffing

500g minced meat (we use half pork, half lamb)

2 eggs, beaten

125g breadcrumbs

40ml milk

1 garlic clove, finely chopped

1 onion, chopped

seasoning

egg wash

salt

Pork loin with rosemary

Ingredients

1 kg loin of pork

1 big bunch of rosemary

2 cloves garlic

75ml rapeseed oil

honey

sea salt

While rare breed pork is becoming very popular in Britain and the rest of Europe, it's not always easy to source here in Ireland. Things are changing, of course, but for the time being we are happy to use the excellent local pork that is supplied by our butcher, Sean Twomey.

Pork is never off the menu and we enjoy its versatility, working with virtually every bit of the pig, from the fillet to the trotters or "crubeens" as we call them here.

Pork has a natural affinity with the barbecue because it has a good layer of fat to retain moisture and if it's cooked slowly and carefully you can have the most wonderful crisp crackling.

I like to slow-roast pork on the barbecue with lots of rosemary, but it's almost as good roasted in the oven - and it's a lot easier to control. But I am a bit of a romantic and that's why I prefer the barbecue. It's a very pure form of cooking and it keeps us in touch with our roots. After all, people were cooking meat this way long before ovens were invented.

For four people you will need to ask your butcher for a loin of pork weighing about 1kg. And ask him to tie the joint up to keep it nice and tight for cooking.

- Pre-heat the oven to 160°C.

- Mash the garlic with a garlic press and add to the oil.

- Season the pork loin with sea salt and rub it with the garlic oil.

- Then slide the rosemary under the string at intervals so as to season the whole piece of meat, leaving 3-4cm between the sprigs.

- Place it on the barbecue and keep the fire low. Alternatively, just pan-fry it briefly on all sides and put in the oven and cook for 10 minutes per 100g, i.e. 1 hour 40 minutes for a loin weighing 1kg.

- On the barbecue the pork must be turned regularly over a low heat for at least two hours until cooked through. You will need to use a meat thermometer to check that the core temperature has reached at least 68°C.

- Before serving remove the rosemary, sprinkle with honey and season with black pepper.

- Serve with potato salad (see page 61).

Free-range pork fillet

with prawns, radish, chard and caramel

Ingredients

4 x 180g pork fillets

rapeseed oil

butter

8 prawns, cleaned and shelled

4 Swiss chard leaves

zest of ½ lemon,
Szechuan pepper, sea salt

caul fat, washed and rinsed
in running cold water

12 fresh round radishes

4 sheets of filo pastry

240g Swiss chard tartare
(see page 58)

mustard leaves

12 fresh round radishes

Prawn caramel

200g sugar

125ml prawn stock

½ tsp Szechuan pepper

1 cardamom pod

- Pre-heat the oven to 175°C.
- Cut the pork fillets down the centre and open them out.
- Rub the inside with rapeseed oil, lemon zest and seasonings.
- Place the Swiss chard leaves on top and place two prawn tails lengthways on top of it.
- Season again.
- Close up tightly.
- Take a piece of caul fat and squeeze the water out of it.
- Spread out and sprinkle with salt.
- Place the rolled up pork fillet in the centre and roll it as tightly as possible in caul fat.
- Cut away the caul fat from the ends.
- Put some oil and a knob of butter in a pan and brown the pork on all sides.
- Transfer to the oven for 12 minutes.
- Remove from oven and rest for 3 minutes in a warm place.
- Slice off the two ends and cut in half.

Prawn caramel

- Dissolve the sugar in a little water.
- Cook to a caramel.
- Put the spices in the prawn stock and heat through.

- When the caramel goes from light to dark brown remove from heat.
- Very carefully add the prawn stock to the caramel and simmer until combined.
- Strain and spoon over the pork.

Swiss chard rolls

- Spread out a sheet of filo pastry.
- Brush with some rapeseed oil.
- Sprinkle with salt, and place 60g of Swiss chard tartare on each.
- Roll up tightly.
- Deep-fry until crisp and golden.
- Remove the ends and slice each roll in three.

Radishes

- Stir-fry the radishes in a very hot pan until warmed through.
- Sprinkle with sea salt, pepper and lemon zest.
- Put on top of the chard rolls and dress with mustard leaves.

Coddle

Ingredients

4 carrots, washed, peeled
and cut in chunks

3 parsnips, washed, peeled and
cut in chunks

3 onions, washed, peeled and
cut in chunks

12 sausages

12 rashers of unsmoked streaky bacon

1 garlic clove

10 potatoes washed, peeled and
cut in chunks

1 sprig of thyme

1.5 ltr chicken stock

butter

I had never heard of coddle until I came to Ireland. A very traditional Dublin dish, it has not travelled outside the country. When Philip joined the team in the summer of 2008 he introduced me to it. After working for several years on cruise ships, he wanted some solid ground under his feet and we were lucky enough to have him land in Ardmore.

Philip is a Dubliner and he has a big personality. He is always cheerful and he is always there when you need him. We got him started in the bar kitchen but he proved himself so quickly that he is now working on the restaurant side of the operation.

When he was here first, his chef jackets became legendary amongst the team. He had to go off to see the housekeeping people for a crash course in ironing. His ironing technique has become less creative and more conventional in the meantime. Oh well, you can only have so many talents and this man can really, really cook.

One day he cooked coddle for staff. Now I have to admit that I was more than a bit surprised to see sausages and rashers in a pot with some potatoes and onions. It looked as if it had been just thrown together and so I tasted with a lot of trepidation.

Wow! What a surprise. It tasted great. Philip explained that this is true, traditional Dublin coddle and that while it doesn't look very attractive, it is unique. He's right. I apologised for jumping to conclusions and making some rather impolite comments before tasting.

Coddle is as good to taste as it is easy to make.

- Melt the butter in a pot and soften the onions over a medium heat.

- Add the sausages and bacon; allow to cook but not to colour.

- Add the stock, thyme, garlic, potato, parsnip and carrots.

- Simmer for 25-30 minutes.

- Season to taste and serve.

Spiced beef with grilled lettuce

and butter dressing

Ingredients

2 medium butterhead or cos lettuces

100g butter

1 lemon

1 tsp each chopped capers, gherkins, shallot and parsley

4 free-range eggs

70g peppered beef per person, sliced as thinly as you can

Our friends at St Raphael's have been growing lettuce for years. Everyone needs lettuce because everyone wants salad. But when we joined forces with them we encouraged the growers here to look beyond the usual varieties, and in Ireland that means the category known as butterhead, the standard issue lettuce with which everyone has grown up. And the people at St Raphael's rose to the challenge.

Even if you can't have a vegetable garden of your own, you can grow your own salad in trays and window boxes, pretty well anywhere at all. If you have even the tiniest garden, you're sorted.

With salad, freshness is everything. Even if your salad mixture is a bit dull, it will taste great if it's really fresh and properly seasoned with some sea salt and black pepper and dressed with good olive oil.

There's nothing wrong with butterhead lettuce, even if it's the salad that we all know so well. Have you ever tried it warm from the barbecue? The charcoal flavour and the tender, sweet, bitter salad leaves work brilliantly together. Serve it with a butter dressing, a poached egg and peppered beef and it really will be a dish you will never forget.

- Fill a large pan with 5cm of water. Add a pinch of salt and a dash of vinegar to help set the eggs. Bring the water to a gentle boil.

- Crack the eggs individually into a cup or ramekin and then gently tip it into the boiling water.

- After 5 minutes carefully remove the poached eggs from the boiling water using a slotted spoon.

- Melt the butter in a pan and let it turn light brown; then add the shallots, capers, gherkins, parsley and a squeeze of lemon juice; set aside.

- Barbecue the halved lettuce heads over a moderate heat and turn them a few times until they are warmed through.

- Then slice in two and cover with the butter mixture.

- Put each half on a plate with a poached egg and the peppered beef.

- To finish, drizzle some of the remaining dressing around with black pepper and lemon zest.

Fillet of beef

with Kilbeggan whiskey

Whiskey and beef. They were certainly two of things that I associated with Ireland even before I decided to come here. Irish beef is probably the best in the world but you have to know what you are looking for. Irish whiskey is amazing stuff and many of the most famous names, like Powers and Jameson, are distilled in Midleton, only half an hour away from The Cliff House.

Our beef is local and comes from Michael McGrath whose little shop in the small town of Lismore is a place of pilgrimage for many people who love good food and who appreciate the real craft of a proper butcher. When we get beef fillets from him we trim them into lovely round pieces and the trimmings are braised overnight.

Cooking fillet steak or sirloin is never easy, because just like preparing eggs for breakfast, everybody has their own idea as to when it is cooked. It's a very personal thing and people get quite upset if they don't get their steak exactly as they want it. This means that a kitchen like ours has to meet the personal requirements of a whole range of customers.

Very often people ask for their steak "well done" and this is the easiest request. You just grill it and put it in the oven and forget about it for 25 minutes. It's a terrible thing to do to a steak but the customer is always right. Even when he's wrong. But I don't want to cremate a steak. Ever. So I do well done steak with a difference. And here's how.

A well done steak needs to be cooked slowly. Otherwise it will just dry out and curl up at the edges. And it will get tough. I always prepare a few in advance. I grill the steaks just to brown them and then vaccuum-pack them with a dash of whiskey. Then I cook them for an hour at 62°C and the result is a steak that is completely cooked, but also retains all its flavour and its juices. A quick flash in a hot oven and you have the best well done steak you have ever tasted.

- Pre-heat the oven to 120°C.

- Heat a grill pan.

- Season the beef on both sides and sprinkle with the whiskey.

- Leave to marinate at room temperature for 15 minutes.

- Then grill the beef on both sides until just browned.

- Put in the oven for a maximum 25 minutes or until it is cooked the way you like it.

Ingredients

4 x 180g fillet steaks

4 tsp Kilbeggan Whiskey

Seasoning

Starch:

Potatoes seem to be an Irishman's best friend so you need to get some nice new potatoes such as Queens or Duke of York and boil them in salted water. When they are cooked, just toss them with a generous knob of butter and a handful of chopped flatleaf parsley

Vegetables:

Whatever you like, but they must be fresh, in season and, ideally, local.

Slow-cooked beef cheeks

scallion, grain mustard and potato purée

Ingredients

2 beef cheeks (about 800g)

100g butter

beef or veal stock
(see page 231)

100g flour

2 thyme and rosemary sprigs

2 fresh bay leaves

3 garlic cloves, chopped

4 onions, diced in cubes

2 tbsp grain mustard

200ml red wine

salt, pepper

20 scallions

potato purée (see page 61)

Beef cheeks may not be the most fashionable cut of meat but they are making a comeback. They have a wonderful flavour which is released through slow cooking. In fact, they taste better than fillet and they are a lot cheaper.

- Slice the beef cheeks in half and season.

- Melt butter in a saucepan.

- Roll the cheeks in flour and brown them in the butter.

- When the beef is coloured, add the onions, herbs and garlic.

- Then add 1 tbsp grain mustard and gently cook for 5 minutes.

- Add the red wine and bring to the boil.

- Let the wine reduce by half and then cover the beef with stock.

- Cover and simmer slowly for 4-5 hours until soft and tender.

- Then remove the beef cheeks and put aside.

- Strain the juice, and reduce until shiny and slightly thick.

- Slice the cheeks, return to the saucepan and heat through in the sauce.

- Fry the scallions until softened.

- Re-heat the potato and serve with the beef cheeks and scallions and the rest of the mustard.

Lamb fillet, herb crust

root vegetables and purple basil

Ingredients

Lamb

4 x 180g lamb fillets

1 tbsp each tarragon, chives, parsley, mint, rosemary, thyme, all finely chopped

½ tbsp garlic, finely chopped

100g breadcrumbs

50g butter

1 garlic clove

olive oil

pepper, sea salt

purple basil (if available; use it to flavour the pan juices)

Root vegetables

2 small parsnips, peeled and cut in two

4 slices streaky bacon rashers, halved lengthwise

8 baby carrots, peeled

½ celeriac, peeled and quartered

2 sweet potatoes, peeled and quartered

olive oil, lemon, pepper, sea salt, rosemary

People are obsessed with the idea of spring lamb and it's true that in the past there was a particular window of opportunity for eating young lamb. But these days lamb is produced throughout the year so it's not as strictly seasonal as it used to be. As far as we are concerned, if it's a lamb, and it's milk-fed and 12 weeks old, we're happy. Spring, summer, autumn or winter lamb, if it meets these requirements, that's fine by us.

Lambs disappear from the fields over the coldest part of the winter, so when they reappear, from being kept inside and away from the frosts, in the spring, people say "Oh, spring lamb!"

However, there will be a difference in taste depending on how the animal has been fed - either inside, or grazing on grass, on the uplands or on coastal shores.

Our lamb is always as local as possible. The local lambs get the best of both worlds, grazing the lush pastures that are more inland, and the strips along the coast where the vegetation is more sparse but the plants are more varied. It's a system that produces the best possible lamb. Irish coastal lamb is unique and we are very lucky to have it.

So much so, it's never off the menu.

- Pre-heat the oven to 170°C.

- Blanch the root vegetables for 2 minutes in boiling water.

- Strain and marinate with some olive oil, rosemary leaves, lemon zest, pepper and sea salt.

- Roll the rashers around the celeriac and parsnip pieces and secure.

- Put all of the vegetables on a baking tray and roast for 25 minutes.

- Melt butter in a pan.

- Mix the herbs with the breadcrumbs, chopped garlic and salt to taste and 2 tbsp of olive oil.

- Season the lamb fillets and crush the garlic clove.

- When the butter is golden brown, add the crushed garlic and the lamb fillets. Brown the fillets on both sides.

- Remove the lamb from the pan and roll through the breadcrumb mixture.

- Put in the oven and cook for 10 minutes with the vegetables. When the vegetables are cooked and the lamb is cooked to your liking, serve immediately sprinkled with olive oil and lemon zest.

Lamb shank

Ingredients

4 lamb shanks

2 sprigs of thyme

1 garlic clove

3 onions, finely chopped

2 carrots, peeled and cut in 2cm slices

½ turnip, peeled and finely diced

2 leeks, cut in 3cm slices

4 potatoes, peeled and quartered

1 ltr vegetable stock

butter, flour, sea salt, black pepper, bay leaves

If ever we need reminding that the cheaper and humbler cuts of meat are often the ones with the best flavour, we need only look at lamb shanks. They really do taste better than the fillet and the rack but, of course, they need to be treated differently.

The shank is also my first choice for Irish stew. I know that everybody has their own version - it's like any classic dish, there are as many versions as there are cooks - but I don't think you can surpass the shank for sheer taste.

We probably should not tell you this but the Irish stew that we serve at The Cliff House - and we think it's the best, to be honest - is just not possible in a domestic kitchen. But the way we do it is interesting.

First we brown the lamb shank on a charcoal grill and then season it with sea salt, thyme and black pepper. Then it's vacuum packed with a little water from cooking the potatoes and a little garlic and then cooked at 68°C for 17 hours. The result is magical, the lamb transformed into a juicy, tender and aromatic bomb. The meat is cooked in a way that the structure is like fillet and the colour deep and intense pink. The juice is used to cook the vegetables and all is served in a deep plate with fresh chopped parsley.

Now, here's the home version. Ideally, you will need a barbecue.

- Pre-heat the oven to 140°C.

- Put the lamb shanks on the barbecue and brown them on all sides. You can always use a domestic grill for this but you will miss out on the smoky flavour.

- Dust them with flour and season.

- Put a casserole on a medium heat and add 2 tbsp of butter.

- Add the garlic, thyme, onions and bay leaves.

- Add the lamb shanks, the vegetables and potatoes.

- Pour in the vegetable stock and bring to a soft boil.

- Cover with tin foil and put in the oven.

- Cook overnight or for at least 12 hours.

- Remove the foil and check the seasoning. Serve.

Sorbets and ice cream

Ice cream has universal appeal. We take it seriously at The Cliff House, to the extent that we always make our own. And we make two kinds, both the usual sweet version and some savoury ones. And we do the same with sorbets.

We make sorbets with celeriac, morels, piccalilli, red cabbage, chocolate and Helvick oysters. We make ice cream with grain mustard, chicken liver, cured ham and juniper berries. They can cause some surprise but, although we say so ourselves, they are absolutely fabulous.

But how do we do it? Normally you have to use sugar to get the right texture. This is because sugar does not freeze and it ensures that you can churn the ice without crystallizing. We have two options. The first is using glycerine, at a rate of 1g glycerine to substitute for 5g of sugar.

The second option only applies if you are lucky enough to have a Pacojet at your disposal. This clever machine scrapes your frozen mixture at very high speed, to produce the right texture. It even has an attachment that allows you to make virtual snow.

Sweet ice cream:
This is familiar territory. But even when we are dealing with normal ice creams and sorbets we work a little differently. For sorbets the classical thing to do is to make a simple syrup and add this in 1:1 ratio to your fruit purée. It certainly works, but you are basically diluting the fruit with a load of water. We dissolve the sugar directly in the fruit purée and then churn the sorbet. It also means you know exactly how much sugar is in it.

Fruits vary enormously in their natural sugar content. For example lemons have 2% sugar, raspberries and strawberries around 7%, apples and cherries around 14%. With that knowledge you can adjust your recipe, bearing in mind that the ideal sugar content is somewhere between 25% and 35%. In our kitchen we can measure the sugar content by using a refractometer which expresses the proportion in terms of the Brix scale (which is the same as the way winemakers determine the ripeness of grapes).

If I want to give the sorbet a more creamy texture I add some gelatine which expands during the churning of the ice and makes the texture richer and smoother.

In making sweet ice creams you will need 320g of sugar to every litre of liquid. In addition to its role in creating the appropriate texture, sugar can be used as carrier for flavour.

Put one vanilla pod and the zest of half a lemon in a blender and add sugar until you have a smooth mixture. Then add yoghurt and blend for five more seconds and you will have a perfectly infused vanilla lemon yoghurt ice base.

Sorbets and ice cream

Savoury sorbet:

Piccalilli sorbet
This is delicious with smoked fish or
cured meats.

250g piccalilli (see page 210)
250ml cauliflower water (200ml water
cooked with 75g cauliflower)
32g glycerine or 160g sugar
salt to taste, zest of ½ lemon

- Mix all ingredients together and churn
  to a smooth sorbet.

Savoury ice cream:

Grain mustard ice cream
We serve this with a green cabbage soup
with roasted garlic and bacon.
450ml milk
50g grain mustard
70g egg yolk
12g glycerine or 70g sugar

- Mix the ingredients together except the
  egg yolks.
- Bring to the boil and pour, whisking all the
  time, on to the egg yolk.
- Return to a low heat and keep whisking
  for another minute.
- Then cool rapidly and churn.

Juniper ice cream
500ml milk
300ml cream
20g glycerine or 100g sugar
80g glucose
30g juniper berries, crushed
20ml dry gin

- Crush the juniper berries and mix all
  components for the ice cream.
- Put in a saucepan and bring to a soft boil.
- Turn down the heat and simmer for
  10 minutes.
- Strain the mixture and put into an ice
  cream machine to churn.

Sweet sorbet:

Raspberry sorbet
500ml raspberry purée made from
fresh raspberries
(If you buy your purée check the label
for sugar content.)
125g fine caster sugar
zest of ¼ lemon and a small pinch of salt
(salt enhances the flavour)

- Mix everything together in a blender
  and churn the sorbet.

Lemon sorbet
This is a strange recipe in that it produces
something half way between a sorbet and
an ice cream.

175ml lemon juice
200ml white wine
140g sugar
60ml milk
60ml cream
½ leaf of gelatine, soaked in cold water
zest of 2 lemons

- Bring the white wine to the boil and
  dissolve the gelatine in it.
- Then add the sugar, cream and milk and
  whisk until dissolved. Cool.
- Add the lemon juice and the zest with
  a pinch of salt. Churn.

Sweet ice cream:

Basil and yoghurt ice cream
This is a lovely confection, blending a very
fragrant herb with sugar to infuse the yoghurt.
In summer it goes well with any red fruits but
is perfect just on its own.

500ml yoghurt
175g sugar
bunch of basil leaves

- Mix the sugar and basil in a blender to
  produce a paste.
- Add the yoghurt and blend until smooth.
- Churn.

Vanilla ice cream
450ml milk
150ml cream
6 egg yolks, beaten
170g sugar
1 vanilla pod

- Mix the vanilla and sugar in a blender.
- Add milk and mix for a few seconds more.
- Combine with the cream and bring to
  a simmer.
- Add the egg yolks and whisk it thoroughly
  for 3-4 minutes on very low heat.
- Strain and cool the mixture.
- Churn.

The variations are endless. Instead of
the vanilla you can use a cinnamon stick,
cardamom or even ground nutmeg. For a
white coffee ice cream, heat 1 tbsp of coffee
beans in a pan and pour over the milk, cream
and sugar. Infuse for 10 minutes, strain and
continue as above.

White chocolate ice cream
This ice cream is served with rhubarb crumble
tart. The basics stay the same, the only
difference being that you substitute the white
chocolate for the cream. Why? Chocolate is
fat, just like cream, and contains around 50%
sugar. All of this is taken into account in the
following recipe.

The method for making this ice cream is
exactly the same as for the vanilla ice cream.

500 ml milk
150g white chocolate
5 egg yolks, beaten
150g sugar

- Bring the milk to a simmer.
- Chop or grate the white chocolate and
  add to the milk.
- Add sugar and whisk in the egg yolks.
- Whisk thoroughly for 3-4 minutes.
- Strain and cool the mixture.
- Churn.

Desserts

Toasted bread parfait

with warm blackberries

Ingredients

350g cider

4 egg yolks

175g sugar

4 slices of white bread, toasted

350g cream

400g blackberries

125g jam sugar

1 orange

Blackberries, or brambles as they are sometimes called, grow everywhere in rural Ireland and Ardmore is no exception. When you take the cliff walk in late summer or early autumn you will come across acres of them. Those shiny, juicy berries have a flavour all of their own and it's great to capture that and to harness it.

Blackberries may look a little like raspberries but they are much tougher and can withstand harsher handling. In fact, they need to be worked a bit in order to release their flavour. Blackberry jam is one of the greats and a mainstay of breakfast here.

This dish combines hot and cold, sweet and tart, creamy and fruity. Having two contrasting temperatures in one dish is always intriguing.

- Whip the cream until it reaches the consistency of yoghurt.

- Pulverise the toasted bread in a food processor.

- Bring the cider to the boil.

- Whisk the egg yolks with the sugar.

- Carefully pour the boiling cider on to the egg/sugar mixture, whisking all the time.

- Return to a low heat and whisk for another 2 minutes.

- Then turn off the heat and cool the pot in iced water.

- When the egg mixture is cool, mix in the breadcrumbs.

- Fold in the whipped cream.

- Pour the mixture into ramekins or a large cake tin.

- Place in the freezer overnight or, ideally, for 24 hours.

To serve, de-mould the parfaits by placing them briefly in hot water and put each in the centre of a plate.

Squeeze the juice of the orange into a saucepan and add the blackberries along with the sugar. Bring to a quick boil and then let it simmer for 3 minutes.

Then scoop it over and around the parfaits.

Crushed strawberries

with tarragon and eggy bread

When I took charge as chef at The Cliff House Hotel in October 2007, there was no kitchen. The place was a building site and my office was a shed. But the main thing that concerned me was the question of getting a garden to supply at least some of our vegetables, fruit and herbs the following year. It weighed on my mind and everybody was worried about just getting all the building work done.

Then I met Willie. He was selling vegetables on the side of the road, not far from Youghal. Suddenly, it occurred to me that this man might be the answer to my prayers. I bought some of his produce, found it very good, and the next time I saw him, I asked him straight. Would he grow vegetables for us at The Cliff House?

And the answer came back without hesitation. No! The fact is that Willie was and is perfectly happy doing just what he has always done and he has neither the time or the inclination to grow stuff for us.

But the one crop that Willie really excels at is strawberries. And we buy pretty well as much as he can grow. We just wish he could grow more because we think his strawberries are the best.

And the best way to eat the best strawberries is at room temperature with whipped cream.

If you really want to do something with strawberries, here's a very simple recipe that is, as they say, more than the sum of its parts.

- Whisk the egg with the sugar, milk and vanilla until the mixture is smooth.

- Heat a non-stick pan over a low heat and melt a knob of butter.

- Put the bread in the egg mixture and let it absorb as much as possible.

- Fry the soaked bread in the pan until golden brown on both sides.

- Clean the strawberries and put them in a bowl.

- Add the tarragon leaves, sugar, zest and juice of the lemon to the strawberries.

- Crush the fruit with a fork.

- Put the golden brown eggy bread on warmed plates and spoon on the strawberries.

- Serve with a scoop of vanilla ice cream or some clotted cream.

Ingredients

500g strawberries

1 small bunch tarragon

juice and zest of 1 lemon

1 tbsp sugar

4 slices white bread

100ml milk

1 tbsp sugar

1 free-range egg

½ tsp vanilla essence

butter

Strawberry collection

Our local strawberries are superb. They have a proper, old-fashioned flavour and they are so popular at The Cliff House that they are never off the menu when they are in season.

This is a kind of celebration of the essence of strawberries and it's constantly getting better the more we cook it. In a sense, it's a kind of template and the chefs here can play around with it, improving it, changing it.

It's as good to look at as it is to eat and it's also a reminder that strawberries can offer varying textures.

This recipe reflects the seven components that we were working with in early July but there are all sorts of options you can try. To give you just some idea, in the meantime I have experimented with tea-smoked strawberries that were grilled on the barbecue. And I made imitation caviar from them too! The possibilities are as endless as your imagination.

But even one or two of the components will be great on their own, of course.

These are the components:

1. Strawberry stock with mint froth
2. Marinated strawberry with 24 carat gold
3. Strawberry fritters
4. Dried strawberry chips
5. Strawberry sorbet
6. Strawberry and caramel
7. Frozen strawberry purée

Strawberry stock and mint froth

- To 300g of the ripest strawberries add 25g of sugar and the zest of ¼ lemon.
- Put in a food processor and purée.
- Put the purée in a clean kitchen towel and squeeze out the liquid.
- Catch the liquid and pour it into four little shot glasses. Chill.
- The remaining purée will be frozen.
- To make the mint froth, take 100ml of cold mint tea, sweeten with sugar and add 0.5g lecithin. Use a hand-held blender to foam it up.

Marinated strawberry

- Crush 200g of strawberries with black pepper, a teaspoon of malt vinegar and 2 basil leaves.
- Spread evenly in a square mould and cover with a sheet of 24 carat gold leaf.

Strawberry fritters

- Mix 3 tbsp of flour with 1½ tbsp of beer and ½ tsp of baking powder until you have a smooth batter.
- Dip 8 strawberries in the mixture and ensure they are well covered.
- Deep-fry until golden brown.
- Dust with icing sugar.

Strawberry chips

- Remove the stalk of the strawberry and cut the remainder into the finest slices possible.
- Spread the slices out on baking paper and put them in the oven at the coolest setting, checking every half hour until they are done.

Strawberry sorbet

- Blend 500g of cleaned strawberries together with 170g of sugar.
- Churn in an ice cream maker until frozen, smooth and creamy in texture.

Strawberry and caramel

- Clean four nice big strawberries and put each on a wooden toothpick.
- Make caramel by dissolving 50g of sugar in a little water. Heat in pan until it turns golden brown.
- Carefully dip the tip of each strawberry in the caramel.
- Withdraw and let the caramel set.

Frozen strawberry purée

- Take the strawberry purée and blend again with 50ml mineral water and juice of an orange.
- Add sugar to taste and pour into rectangular freezer bags or trays and freeze.

Carrageen pudding

with raspberries, soda bread and basil

Ingredients

450ml organic milk

50g sugar

4g carrageen moss (dried)

¼ bunch basil

250g raspberries

2 slices brown soda bread

2 tsp Golden Syrup

lemon zest

This is a very light and unusual treat for anyone who has a passion for desserts. It's wholly Irish, very traditional and remarkably easy to prepare. I first ate it at Ballymaloe House, where traditional Irish food is really showcased, and was intrigued by the silky texture that the carrageen moss produces. Actually, it's not a moss at all. It's a seaweed which in Gaelic is called "little rock". Brown sugar is the traditional accompaniment.

You can get carrageen in most healthfood shops and some fishmongers stock it. If you can't find any, it can be replaced with vegetable gelatine. But of course the texture will be a little different.

Anyway, this is the version of this truly authentic Irish pudding that we serve at The Cliff House.

Raspberries are best but you can use any soft fruit.

- Soak the carrageen in cold water for at least 10 minutes.

- Warm the milk with the sugar and the stalks of the basil.

- Crumble the soda bread onto an oven tray and sprinkle with the Golden Syrup.

- Place in the oven at 170°C until slightly caramelised.

- Remove the carrageen from the water and squeeze the water out.

- Add to the warm milk mixture and let it simmer with a lid on.

- After 15 minutes, strain the mixture and push the carrageen through a fine sieve.

- Put aside three raspberries per person.

- Mix the remaining raspberries with some small basil leaves and divide between four glasses.

- Pour the carrageen mixture on top.

- Let set in the fridge for at least 45 minutes.

- Slice the rest of the basil leaves as finely as possible and mix with the soda bread crumbs.

- Spread the crumb mixture over the surface of each pudding and then grate over some lemon zest.

- Top each with three raspberries, a basil leaf and serve.

Gooseberry fool

Gooseberries must be the most under-appreciated fruit in the world. Maybe people are just put off by that incredible tartness, the breathtaking acidity that remains even when they are super-ripe. But they are fantastic.

Our friend Mrs Nugent brings us gooseberries from her own garden and she always stops for a chat about the good life in Ireland and what she is harvesting. She introduced me to this phenomenal fruit with its pungency, its tartness and its utterly unique flavour.

When May gives way to June, that's when the first of the gooseberries are ready. Some varieties turn from green to something approaching yellow when fully ripe, others turn red and become softer and juicier.

We often serve a little gooseberry fool at the end of dinner at The Cliff House, just as a little reminder of the childhood taste of this very Irish fruit and also because it's so light, refreshing and cleansing.

The base is a gooseberry marmalade.

Gooseberry marmalade

- Remove stalks and any remains of the flowers and rinse the gooseberries in cold water.

- Put in a pot with the orange juice.

- Bring slowly to the boil and add the sugar.

- Simmer for 15-20 minutes and then add the orange zest.

- Check the consistency by dipping with a spoon; if the back of the spoon is covered, the right consistency has been reached.

- Spoon into a jam jar and close it: turn the jar upside down to create a vacuum.

- Turn right side up after 10 minutes and store in a dark and cool place.

Fool

- Take 100g of gooseberry marmalade and use a blender to turn it into a smooth paste.

- Put in a mixing bowl and add 2 egg whites.

- Whisk until the mixture becomes fluffy.

- Spoon a thin layer of gooseberry marmalade into the bottom of a serving glass.

- Spoon the fool on top.

- Garnish with zest of lemon and finely sliced mint leaves.

Ingredients

500g fully ripe gooseberries

200g jam sugar

zest and juice of 1 orange

2 egg whites

lemon zest

mint leaves

Custard

Is there anyone who doesn't like custard? Every country seems to have its own version, always somehow based on milk and eggs, and called lots of different things.

It's fashionable to call it crème and proper old-fashioned Irish custard is sometimes called crème anglaise. Well, not here it isn't! There are three ways to make custard, the first two being semi-solid; the third creamy and liquid.

- In a ramekin standing in a water bath in a cool oven.
- In a tart as filling.
- In a saucepan, constantly stirred.

And of course, there are sweet and savoury versions. In the past, especially in medieval times, custard was used as a filling or binding agent in tarts and flans. This, in fact, is how it got its name, custard being a corruption of "crustade", meaning a pie with a crust.

At The Cliff House we make our own custard and, as with a lot of standard recipes, we play with the ingredients but respect the basic recipe.

Basic custard:
500ml milk
3 whole eggs, beaten
2 egg yolks
120g sugar

- Mix all the ingredients together in a saucepan.
- Gently heat the mixture, stirring constantly.
- When the mixture thickens and little bubbles start to come to the surface, the custard is cooked.
- Strain through a fine sieve and place in the fridge to cool.
- To prevent skin forming lay a sheet of butter paper on top.

This is the most basic sweet custard. Serve it with soaked prunes or use it to create a trifle.

Honey and cream custard:
250ml milk
250ml cream
6 egg yolks
150g honey

- Pre-heat the oven to 120°C.
- Mix all ingredients together and divide between 4 ramekins.
- Put them on the middle shelf of the oven.
- After 45 minutes check the the custards by shaking them gently. If any of it is still jiggling then it needs a bit longer; the custards are cooked when the centre sets.

- Remove from oven and put in the fridge to cool and set for at least 2 hours.
- Dress the top with raspberries or other soft fruits and serve or just sprinkle it with a thin layer of sugar and slowly caramelise it with a blowtorch until golden and crisp.

Chocolate custard:
350ml milk
150ml cream
150g chocolate (dark or milk)
100g sugar
5 egg yolks
1 tsp cocoa powder

- Bring the milk and the cream to a soft boil.
- Grate in the chocolate and let it dissolve.
- Mix the egg yolks, cocoa powder and sugar to a smooth paste.
- Pour the hot mixture on top of it and stir well until it is completely combined.

Now, there are three options:
- Cook the custard on low heat in a pot.
- Cook the custard in a ramekin or other mould.
- Cook the custard in a tart base.

Caramelised cream with raspberries

Ingredients

fresh raspberries

570ml cream

2 vanilla pods

4 egg yolks

110g caster sugar

Adriaan Bartels is the General Manager at The Cliff House Hotel and, as such, he has done a huge amount to create the unique place that it is. He has a mental flexibility and total unflappability that I really envy.

Adriaan and I always seem to be on the same wavelength. Maybe it's because of our shared Dutch background.

I am privileged to work with him. We both know how to argue our case and fight our corner. And we don't like losing! But we have the same goals in sight.

Without Adriaan I couldn't do what I do at The Cliff House. This recipe is by him.

Bedankt Adriaan!

- Split the vanilla pods and scrape the seeds into the cream along with the pods.

- Combine the egg yolks with the sugar and whisk.

- Heat the cream until boiling.

- Add to the yolk mixture, mix and strain.

- Return the mixture to a clean pan and place on a low heat, stirring continuously until it thickens.

- Do not let the mixture boil.

- Pour this mixture into ramekins in which you have placed a layer of raspberries.

- Place in the refrigerator overnight.

- Before serving dust the top of the mixture with caster sugar, then, using a blow torch, caramelise the top until golden brown and it forms a sugar crust.

Flourless chocolate tart

candied orange and whiskey cream

This very rich chocolate dessert is sometimes called Chocolate Nemesis which is apt because the dictionary defines a nemesis as "one who exacts vengeance". It certainly does if you happen to be on a diet or even just slightly concerned about counting calories. "Nemesis" can also be construed as "downfall". That seems pretty apt too.

There is no need for flour in the recipe – something that comes as a surprise to many people – because the four ingredients combine to produce a filling so intense, so wickedly rich that any addition would be superfluous.

Or would it? They are not really additions, and they really enhance the dish, so we serve our Chocolate Nemesis in our bar restaurant with candied orange and whiskey cream.

The limited number of ingredients is reflected in the simplicity of the method.

- Pre-heat the oven to 160°C.
- Melt the butter and chocolate over a low heat.
- Whisk the eggs with the sugar until you have the consistency of raw meringue mixture.
- Fold into the chocolate mixture until completely smooth and blended.
- Fill the baking tin with this mixture.
- Bake for 30 minutes.
- The chocolate tart is cooked when the crust is crisp and the mixture has set.
- Take from the oven and carefully remove the ring.
- Cool and let stand for at least 2-3 hours.
- Then cut and serve, bearing in mind how rich it is.
- If you want you can place the tart in the fridge, cut it when chilled, and then let it come up to room temperature before serving.

To make the whiskey cream, whisk 250ml cream with 50ml of whiskey and a teaspoon of brown sugar until it reaches the consistency of yoghurt. It can be prepared in advance and kept in the fridge.

To make the candied orange, thinly slice 2 oranges into rings, then boil them in sugar syrup until they are impregnated with sugar and thoroughly glazed.

Ingredients

300g dark chocolate, broken into small pieces

270g sugar

5 eggs

250g butter

A 24cm baking tin with removable ring, buttered

Chocolate mousse with olive oil

and sea salt, pistachio and coffee ice cream

Ingredients

250g dark chocolate

80g sugar

120ml egg white

320ml cream

4 tbsp roasted pistachio nuts

Maldon sea salt

olive oil

There is no doubt about it. Chocolate makes you feel good. It contains natural chemicals that are mood enhancers and nobody is very surprised to hear it. Chocolate is ubiquitous, especially in restaurants.

At The Cliff House we use chocolate in as many ways as you can imagine, from lollipops and mousses, tarts and drinks, to savoury sauces. With chocolate, there are few boundaries.

Milk chocolate with lobster may sound weird but, believe me, it works. More conventionally, I have also used dark chocolate to give greater depth to a beef or game sauce.

Less conventionally, I like to serve white chocolate and juniper ice cream with local pigeon.

Here we have a dessert with a pure, undiluted savoury element as a foil. It's salt. And nothing is more savoury than that.

This is a real "just try it" dish. It may sound strange, but if you make it and taste you will see what the fuss is about. The rich dark chocolate mousse is sprinkled with Maldon sea salt crystals and it draws out all the deep flavours of the chocolate.

- Whisk the cream until it has the consistency of yoghurt.

- Melt the chocolate in a mixing bowl over warm water.

- Set aside the melted chocolate.

- Whisk the egg whites until stiff and add the sugar, whisking until a nice shine appears.

- Fold this mixture into the melted chocolate.

- Fold the cream into this mixture and mix well.

- Place in the fridge for at least 4 hours.

- Crush the pistachio nuts.

- With a warm spoon place scoops of the mousse on each serving plate and surround with crushed pistachios.

- Place a scoop of coffee ice cream on each plate (see page 179).

- Drizzle a little very good olive oil around each plate.

- Last, but not least, carefully place some sea salt crystals on top of the chocolate mousse.

Upside down pear tart

Ingredients

1 sheet of puff pastry, cut into a round
the size of the pan

5 medium-sized pears, peeled,
cored and quartered

200g sugar (mixed with seeds
of ½ vanilla pod, ½ tsp each of
ground nutmeg and cardamom)

50g butter

70ml water

zest of 1 lemon

Apples and pears are the harbingers of winter. They are also the basis of lots of delicious hearty dishes that help us to cope with the change in the season and the hard weather to come. Autumn is a time when the emphasis changes in the kitchen and we leave behind some of the lighter, almost ethereal, dishes of summer and turn towards something more earthy, maybe less refined.

You can buy pears, like any other fruit or vegetable, at any time of the year but the thought of eating this pear tart with caramel during the summer just would not seem right.

The tart we are making here is our very own version of *tarte tatin*, which of course is originally made with apples. But you can just about get away with using pears and calling it *tarte tatin*. People make *tartes tatins* from just about anything these days, from chicory to onions, so what the hell?

Even though this is basically a simple dish, the recipe is all about patience and really first class ingredients. At The Cliff House we make individual tarts but at home I would suggest making a big one to share with family or friends.

The best *tartes tatins* are made, cooked and eaten at once, served with a generous scoop of vanilla ice cream and a dash of Baileys. You don't hang around with this dish.

You will need a non-stick frying pan with a 24cm base.

- Pre-heat the oven to 175°C.

- Add the sugar mix to the water in the pan.

- Dissolve on a medium heat and then let it come to the point of caramelisation.

- Add the butter and the pears and soften them slowly on a low heat, turning the pears so they are cooked on both sides.

- Make sure the pears are round side down in the caramel and arrange them evenly in the pan.

- Cover with the pastry and press and mould it tight around the pears.

- Then bake until the pastry crust is brown and crisp.

- Remove from the oven and place a large plate on top of the pan/pie.

- Turn it upside down very quickly and remove the pan to reveal the *tarte*.

- Sprinkle the top (which was, until recently, the bottom) with lemon zest.

- Cut into slices and serve directly with vanilla ice cream and Baileys Irish Cream.

Rhubarb crumble tart

lemon curd and ice cream

Ingredients

4 x 10cm sheets of puff pastry

300g rhubarb, cleaned and cut in 1cm slices

80g jam sugar

1 orange

25g sugar

50g butter

75g flour

50g marzipan

1 egg white

1 lemon

butter to grease the tins

vanilla ice cream (see page 179)

Maybe it's the weather but warm desserts are very popular in Ireland and rhubarb is a perennial favourite. You can serve rhubarb in lots of different ways but I keep coming back to the simple, straightforward goodness of this dessert. Our friend Francis provides us with the most beautiful rhubarb I have ever encountered, yet another example of brilliant and delicious local produce. Francis's rhubarb has great texture. It stays firm and juicy no matter what.

This warm rhubarb tart is made with a puff pastry lining and a crumble topping, so there's a nice contrast of textures. The almond paste and lemon help to create a really complete dish with intriguing flavours. You will need four quiche tins 10cm in diameter.

- Pre-heat the oven to 170°C.

- Butter the quiche tins.

- Take the puff pastry and stretch it until it is wide enough to fit in the tins.

- Line carefully and let the pastry overlap the tins slightly.

- Refrigerate.

- Make the crumble mixture: mix the butter with the sugar then rub in the flour until the mixture resembles crumbs.

- Mix marzipan with the egg white and lemon juice and zest.

- Mix the rhubarb with the jam sugar, and the orange juice and zest.

- Now assemble the tarts.

- Divide the marzipan by spooning into the quiche tins.

- Divide the rhubarb by spooning over the marzipan.

- Fold back the outsides of the pastry.

- Fill with crumble mixture.

- Bake for 25-30 minutes.

- Serve with vanilla ice cream and a little lemon curd.

Almond cookies

Daan is an intriguing figure. In some way he's like a sniper, quick, silent, deadly accurate and always on target.

His mother asked for a job for him at De Kas when he was only sixteen. She had decided that he needed some discipline and a proper goal in life.

Having Daan in the kitchen is a great advantage. He understands what I mean and he's great at communicating the details of certain dishes to the other members of the team. When I think of meeting him first when he was sixteen and look at him now it just makes me feel very pleased and rather proud: he's independent, confident and disciplined.

Originally he is from Weesp. The name of that little town has been given to the sweet almond cookies that are delicious with ice cream or as a treat with coffee or tea.

After some heavy negotiations he eventually gave in and decided to share his secret family recipe.

- Pre-heat the oven to 170°C.

- Mix all ingredients by hand in a bowl until smooth.

- Make rolls of this and slice into cookies 2 cm thick.

- Whisk an egg with the cream and use this to brush the cookies twice.

- Sprinkle with the chopped almonds and brush with the egg wash.

- Bake the cookies for 8 minutes until golden brown.

Serve with a fluffy sabayon or with a scoop of your favourite ice cream.

Ingredients

250g marzipan

zest of 1 lemon

zest of 1 orange

1 egg yolk

½ whole egg

30g ground almonds

chopped almonds to finish

egg wash: 1 egg plus 2 tbsp cream

Ardmore carrot cake

Ingredients

250g grated carrot

125g flour

125g butter

175g sugar

75g ground almonds

2 eggs

3 oranges (juice and zest)

1 tsp bicarbonate of soda

½ tsp salt

The area around Ardmore is famous for its carrots and we like to celebrate this in various ways. The carrot is a vegetable, of course, but because of its natural sweetness it is sometimes used in desserts.

When I was a kid, they tried to get me to eat carrots by telling me that they improve your eyesight but I was having none of it. I still don't know if it's true but I hated carrots until I discovered carrot cake. Maybe that's because it's a lovely sweet cake and it doesn't taste like any carrot that I've ever eaten.

At The Cliff House we make mini-versions of carrot cake and serve it with tea and coffee. As a twist we let the guest "inject" it with a carrot syrup at the table so the cake is lovely and soaky and full of extra carrot flavour.

You can also make a big version in a cake tin.

- Pre-heat the oven to 170°C.
- Beat the butter and sugar to a smooth white paste in a mixing bowl.
- One by one, add the eggs. The mixture will split but don't worry, it will work out fine.
- Then add the carrots, orange zest and ground almonds.

- Mix well.
- Mix in the the orange juice.
- Add all the other ingredients: flour, bicarbonate of soda, salt. Mix.
- Put in a cake tin and bake for 35-40 minutes.
- You will know it is cooked when you stick a skewer into the cake and it comes out clean.
- Cool and slice.
- Serve with clotted cream.
- You could glaze the cake with some melted milk chocolate.

Irish cherry olive oil cake

yoghurt and mint

This dessert is not just the very essence of summer, it's also amazingly simple.

The cherries can be replaced by strawberries, raspberries or other fruits but nothing works quite like cherries.

- Pre-heat the oven to 185°C.
- Butter 4 ramekins or a big pie dish.
- Stone the cherries and toss them in the jam sugar and add the orange zest.
- Transfer these to the ramekins or pie dish.
- Mix wine, olive oil, eggs and sugar with a pinch of salt.
- Mix the flour and baking powder and add to the other ingredients and whisk to a smooth batter.

- Continue whisking until the mixture becomes fluffy.
- Cover the cherries with the mixture and sprinkle with the crushed pistachios. Bake for 12-14 minutes if using ramekins or 20-25 minutes for the big version. Test with a skewer. If it comes out clean, the cake is done.
- Remove from oven.
- Slice mint into the thinnest strips possible and add to the yoghurt.
- Serve with a scoop of the yoghurt.

Ingredients

500g cherries

50g jam sugar

orange zest

70g sugar

100ml white wine

90ml olive oil

110g flour

2 eggs

1 tsp baking powder

pinch of salt

crushed pistachios

125ml organic yoghurt

6 mint leaves

Jam, jellies, drinks and preserves

The chutney combines well with rich dishes such as braised meat, grilled fatty fish and, of course, cheese.

Pumpkin Chutney

700g pumpkin, skin and seeds removed,
diced into equal cubes
250g apple, grated
1 tbsp fresh ginger, grated
¼ chilli pepper, finely chopped
200ml vinegar
60g brown sugar
20g jam sugar
1 tsp coriander seeds
½ tsp cloves, crushed
½ tsp black peppercorns, crushed
¼ cinnamon stick
2 star anise
juice and zest of 1 lemon
salt to taste

- Put the pumpkin, apple, vinegar and the chilli into a large pot.
- Add 2 cups of water and bring to the boil.
- Turn down the heat and after 45 minutes add the spices and the sugar.
- Let the chutney simmer until the pumpkin starts to shine and fall apart.
- Add the ginger, lemon juice and zest.
- Simmer for a further 25 minutes, adding water if it becomes too dry.
- Season to taste.
- Spoon into clean preserve jars and seal.
- Turn the jars upside down in order to create a vacuum.
- Turn right side up after 10 minutes and store in a dark and cool place.

The chutney needs to mature for about 2 weeks before it is good to eat, but it can hold for up to a year. After opening, keep it in the fridge.

The chutney combines well with rich dishes such as braised meat, grilled fatty fish and, of course, cheese.

Piccalilli

60g flour
15g ginger powder
80g mustard powder
25g turmeric powder
500ml vinegar
130g sugar
100ml ginger syrup
300g cauliflower rosettes (small)
2 onions, diced in cubes
100g cucumber, diced in cubes
50g carrot, diced in cubes
pepper and salt

- Sweat the onions in a saucepan with a little oil.
- Add the flour, ginger, mustard and turmeric.
- Heat through for 60 seconds and set aside.
- Bring the vinegar to the boil and add the cauliflower rosettes, carrots and cucumber.
- Cook until the cauliflower is tender, then strain. Put the vegetables aside.
- Add the ginger syrup and sugar to the vinegar.

- Pour onto the flour and spice mix and whisk to remove any lumps.
- Simmer this mixture for 10 minutes.
- Add the vegetables and bring to the boil. Simmer for a further 10 minutes.
- Season to taste.
- Put into a clean jar and keep in the fridge.

Jam, jellies, drinks and preserves

Tomato jam

This is super on some crispy garlic bread with some goat's cheese. More unusually, it's really good with vanilla ice cream too...

1 kg ripe tomatoes, quartered
and seeds removed
300g jam sugar
10g pectin
zest of 1 orange
zest and juice of 1 lemon
salt
2 star anise
1 vanilla pod
1 tsp cardamon
½ tsp coriander seeds
½ tsp juniper berries
½ tsp cloves
½ tsp black peppercorns

- Mix the tomatoes with the orange and lemon zest.
- Dry roast the spices gently in a pan for 2 minutes.
- Mix the sugar, pectin and roasted spices in a food processor until the spices are broken up.
- Sieve the sugar on top of the tomatoes.
- Mix with the tomatoes and let the flavours infuse for 1 hour.
- Then bring the mixture to a soft boil.

- Let it cook until the tomatoes become shiny and transparent - about 15 minutes.
- Taste it, add the lemon juice and season to taste.
- Fill pasteurised jars with the hot jam and screw on the lids.
- Turn the jars upside down for 10 minutes so as to create a vacuum.
- Store in a cool, dark place.

Tomato ketchup

At the end of the tomato season comes the glut. We always have masses of them, some over-ripe, some damaged, just loads of tomatoes. This is when we get moving on making soups, sauces, oils and ketchup.

At The Cliff House we make our own even if we know that we will never make enough to keep us going for a whole year. But it's still worth doing, because it's gorgeous and completely different from the commercially made ones.

You need a big pot and a lot of patience, but I promise it will be worth all the effort. And your kids will thank you. Make it once and every time you do it again you will be making little adjustments. So, in the end, you have your very own personal style of ketchup, unique to you.

3 kg ripe tomatos, chopped
200ml vinegar
3 onions, chopped
2 celery stalks, chopped
2 hot peppers, seeds removed, chopped
1 red pepper, seeds removed, chopped
50g grated fresh ginger
1 tbsp mustard
½ tbsp each ground star anise and cloves
3 cloves garlic, finely chopped
250g brown sugar

- Mix all ingredients except the sugar together and put in a large pot.
- Put on a medium heat and bring to the boil.
- When it boils, let it simmer for 1 hour.
- Then, with a hand-held blender, purée the mixture.
- Add the sugar.
- Let it simmer for at least 1 hour.
- Pass through a sieve.
- Then put back on the stove and reduce the ketchup until it thickens.
- Then pour in to clean jars and store the ketchup in the fridge where it will keep for 2 months.

This is super on some crispy garlic bread with some goat's cheese.
More unusually, it's really good with vanilla ice cream too...

Jam, jellies, drinks and preserves

Carrot smoothie

Here's a healthy low fat smoothie which will set you up for the day and deliver lots of essential nutrients.

250ml low fat organic milk
2 carrots, peeled
½ apple, peeled
4 apple mint leaves

- Pour the milk into a blender.
- Dice the carrot and apple.
- Add with the mint to the milk.
- Blend until smooth.
- Pour into a large glass with ice cubes.
- Add some organic honey if you wish.

If you like an ice-cold smoothie you can also freeze the ingredients, other than the milk. For a different version, replace the milk with yoghurt, and the apple with pear or orange. And you could try replacing the mint with basil or lemon balm.

Rhubarb gin

Rhubarb is one of the first signs that winter is over. The forced rhubarb that starts to appear just after Christmas is very delicate both in texture and in colour (which is candy pink). It has a very distinctive flavour and is quite sweet as rhubarb goes.

The first of the ordinary rhubarb shoots forth from the earth in February but it only comes into its own as spring advances. Thanks to a host of different varieties, you can have rhubarb, a vegetable that we all treat as a fruit, right through until May, even later if you're careful.

We make a flavoured gin with the later rhubarb which has a chunkier texture and is not very sweet, very tart actually. It is very different from the ruby-coloured sloe gin that is made from the very bitter little berries that grow on blackthorn bushes in the hedgerows. It makes a lovely summer drink if you dilute it with sparkling water or, better still, sparkling wine. It can also be used as a really special marinade for summer fruits and is especially good poured over ice cream.

This recipe makes a bottle of rhubarb gin. We like to use our local Cork Dry Gin which has a very distinctive flavour (some people claim it has a whiff of ground coffee) but any decent gin will do. You will need one large preserve jar.

500g rhubarb
250g sugar
8 mint leaves
1 bottle Cork Dry Gin

- Cut the rhubarb into small pieces and add the sugar and the mint leaves.
- Mix well and put into the preserve jar.
- Pour the gin on top of the rhubarb. Make sure the jar is filled to the brim.
- Secure the lid and put the jar into a pan of simmering water.
- After 25 minutes take the jar out and shake well.
- Keep the jar at room temperature for at least 10 weeks.
- Shake well again and strain.
- Use a sieve and a ladle to squeeze all the juices out of the rhubarb.
- Pour into a suitable bottle. The gin is now ready.

Jam, jellies, drinks and preserves

Elderflower barley water

The blossom of the elder tree does not appear to be particularly aromatic at first but the moment you apply heat to it the fragrance rises like a volcano. They make wonderful fritters which we sometimes serve with strawberries. The idea is to encase the elderflowers in a thin, frothy, crisp batter and then to deep-fry them briefly until crisp and golden. For me this is heaven on a plate: simple, straightforward and very pure.

I don't think our guests shared my wild enthusiasm but they liked it and found it unusual and just a little challenging. On the other hand, the elderflower and barley water that we served in a test tube looked a bit strange but everybody loved it. It is a perfect palate cleanser and a good way to close a night of dining at The Cliff House.

Of course, it's also very good in a big glass with lots of crushed ice and a slice or two of lemon on a sunny day. It's wonderfully refreshing.

2 ltr water
100g barley
2 lemons
sugar and elderflowers

- Bring water to the boil and add the barley.
- Slice the lemons thinly and add to the boiling water.
- Reduce the heat and simmer for 1 hour.
- Add lots of elderflowers (4-5 big heads).
- Stir and add as much or as little sugar as you wish.
- Cover and turn off the heat.
- When cold, strain and taste.
- If you want it to taste more acidic add lemon juice and zest to taste.
- Bottle and store in the fridge.

This makes a very good jelly for serving with summer fruits.

Take 1 leaf of gelatine for every 100ml elderflower barley water.

- Soak the gelatine in cold water.
- Take a glassful of the elderflower barley water and warm it.
- Put the gelatine in the warm liquid and stir until completely dissolved.
- Strain and add the liquid to the rest of the elderflower barley water.
- Put in a mould and let it set in the fridge for at least 4 hours.
- Put the mould in hot water and turn the jelly out onto a plate.
- Dress with fresh summer fruits and serve.

Jam, jellies, drinks and preserves

It's strange to think that something so seductive and so versatile can be made so simply and so quickly. It literally takes just a few minutes.

Strawberry jam

1 kg strawberries, hulled and halved
500g jam sugar
juice and zest of ½ orange

- Clean jam jars and pasteurise them in a large pot of boiling water.
- Mix the strawberries with the jam sugar and the orange juice.
- Put them on a low heat and then let come to a soft boil.
- Simmer for 15 minutes and add the orange zest.
- Fill the pasteurised jars with the hot jam and screw on the lids.
- Turn the jars upside down for 10 minutes so as to create a vacuum.
- Store in a cool, dark place.

Lemon curd

Lemon curd is so versatile that you can't really afford to be without it. It can act as a glaze for berries, a sauce with ice cream (or a base for ice cream), a filling for a cake or a tart, or it can be enjoyed - relished really - just as it is, with hot buttered toast or scones. But to be worthy of the name, lemon curd has to be tangy, finely coloured, buttery, not too sweet and it has be silky and seductive in texture. It's strange to think that something so seductive and so versatile can be made so simply and so quickly. It literally takes just a few minutes.

Here is the recipe that we use at The Cliff House. It reveals one of our secrets, namely how we get the brilliant colour (we use just a hint of saffron, which also adds an intriguing taste).

2 large free range eggs
160g sugar
pinch of saffron
2 lemons
70g butter

- Find a pot into which a mixing bowl will fit snugly.
- Partly fill with water and place the mixing bowl on top.
- Place on the heat. You will need gentle, indirect heat to bring the curd together. If in doubt, go cooler rather than hotter.
- Put the sugar, eggs and saffron into the mixing bowl and stir.
- Add the zest and juice of the lemons and stir.
- Continue stirring and heating gently until the texture resembles a thin custard.
- Stir in the butter.
- Spoon into jam jars and seal.
- Turn the jars upside down in order to create a vacuum.
- Turn right side up after 10 minutes and store in a dark and cool place.

Orange marmalade

A proper Irish breakfast is never complete without marmalade. It is obviously one of the best things you can have with toast but it's also very good with warm scones and a little cream.

You can't just use any old orange for making marmalade. It needs the high pectin content and the bitterness that you get only with Seville oranges which are available in mid-winter. A good batch of marmalade will keep you going throughout the year but it's still a seasonal item for the kitchen diary.

750g Seville oranges (you can use other unwaxed oranges but it won't taste the same)
1 lemon
500g jam sugar
500g sugar
2 ltr water

- Wash the oranges and pasteurise your jam jars.
- Remove the rind of the oranges with a peeler and reserve.
- Chop the oranges.
- Put in a pot with water and both sugars.
- Put on a low heat and bring to a very gentle boil.
- Cut the orange peel into very thin strips.

- After the oranges have cooked for 30 minutes, purée with a hand blender.
- Add the orange strips and let the marmalade reduce until it thickens.
- Then add the juice and zest of the lemon.
- Check the consistency by putting a spoon in the marmalade. If the back of the spoon comes out coated, the right consistency has been reached.
- Spoon into the jars and close them. Turn the jars upside down in order to create a vacuum.
- Turn the right way up after 10 minutes and store in a dark and cool place.

Raspberry jam

Raspberries are an integral part of summer. They are also, in many ways, the supreme red fruit with their intense flavour and bracing acidity. They are worth waiting for. It is usually into July by the time the summer crop is ready for picking but the autumn varieties can go on well into October.

They are best eaten just on their own, maybe with a little sugar, perhaps with some cream. At The Cliff House, that's how we like to approach raspberries, by doing as little to them as possible. If they are over-ripe or damaged we use them in sauces, ice creams or jams.

Jam, jellies, drinks and preserves

All the jams and marmalades at The Cliff House are made on the premises because we just don't like the commercial versions which are so sweet and all too often very short on actual fruit.

Making your own jams and preserves is very satisfying work and if you use your freezer you can spread the work over many months rather than engaging in a frenzy of jam making at the height of the harvest.

The base of a good jam is always sound, ripe fruit.

1 kg over-ripe raspberries
400g jam sugar
½ lemon (zest and juice)
1 mint tea bag

- Clean jam jars and pasteurise them in a large pot of boiling water.
- Mix the raspberries with the jam sugar and the lemon juice in a large pot.
- Bring to a soft boil.
- Simmer for 10 minutes and add the mint tea bag.
- Remove tea bag after 1 minute (or leave it longer if you would like to have more mint flavour).
- Add the lemon zest.

- Fill the pasteurised jars with the raspberry jam and screw the lids on.
- Turn the jars upside down so as to create a vacuum.
- Turn right side up after 10 minutes and store in a dark and cool place.

Blackberry and orange fruit cube
500g blackberry purée
750g sugar
18g pectin
5g cream of tartar
2 oranges, juice and zest
more sugar

- Juice and zest the oranges.
- Combine the purée and the juice.
- Bring to the boil.
- Mix the sugar with the pectin and add this to the boiling fruit mixture.
- Cook for 20-25 minutes, stirring frequently.
- Dissolve the cream of tartar in a little water and add to the mixture.
- Now add the orange zest.
- Cook for a further 5 minutes then pour into a rectangular container in which it can set.
- Leave overnight.
- Unmould the set purée and slice into cubes.
- Roll in sugar and serve.

Strawberry and black pepper fruit cube

500g strawberry purée
700g sugar
20g pectin
6g cream of tartar
2 tsp black pepper, freshly ground
more sugar

- Bring the purée to the boil.
- Mix the sugar with the pectin and add
  to the boiling fruit purée.
- Cook for 20-25 minutes, stirring frequently.
- Dissolve the cream of tartar in a little water
  and add to the mixture.
- Cook for a further 5 minutes, add the
  pepper, then pour into a rectangular
  container in which it can set.
- Leave overnight.
- Unmould the set purée and slice
  into cubes.
- Roll in sugar and serve.

Pear and butter mash

500g whole ripe pears, peeled
150g jam sugar
¼ nutmeg
40g butter

- Cut the pears in pieces, including
  the cores.
- Mix with the sugar.
- Put on a low heat.
- Cook slowly until the pears start to break up.

- Grate in the nutmeg and add the butter.
- Put in a food processor and blend into
  a purée.
- Pass it through a sieve and check the
  consistency; if it is a bit runny just return
  to the heat and let it thicken.
- Then pour it into a jam jar and keep in
  the fridge until use.

Lemon and mint tea fruit cube

450ml lemon juice
50g lemon zest
800g sugar
20g pectin
6g cream of tartar
2 mint tea bags

- Bring the lemon juice and zest to the boil.
- Add the mint tea bags and let them infuse
  for 3-4 minutes; then remove.
- Mix the sugar and pectin and add to the
  lemon mixture.
- Cook for 20 minutes, stirring frequently.
- Dissolve the cream of tartar in a little water
  and add to the mixture.
- Cook for a further 5 minutes then pour into
  a rectangular container in which it can set.
- Leave overnight.
- Unmould the set purée and slice into cubes.
- Roll in sugar and serve.

From London to Amsterdam:

with a lot of relief

There's something really nice about a restaurant in a park. De Kas is in a restored greenhouse in a public park just outside the centre of Amsterdam. I left London with a lot of relief and went there as head chef when it opened.

It has a barbecue for chargrilling and when you are walking through the park you can catch the smell of it, that lovely savoury smell, so that it's a kind of aperitif that you inhale in the fresh air.

De Kas was opened in 2001 and is the brain-child of Gert Jan Hageman, who found the derelict greenhouse, part of the former city plant nursery, and decided that it could become a restaurant with a difference. "It seems an obvious concept," he says, "but I spent twenty years surrounded by white tiles under fluorescent lighting before I came up with it. Daylight shines in from all sides, the chefs are free to express their creativity daily, using the best that the season has to offer. It's a kitchen surrounded by fertile soil where vegetables and herbs thrive…"

The whole idea behind De Kas was, and still is, to limit, as far as possible, the amount of time it takes to get from the harvest to the diner's plate. It's also about genuine simplicity because the quality of raw materials is so good. The restaurant has two vegetable gardens, one on-site, the other close by, and the building itself, dating from the 1920s, is remarkable. It had been due for demolition but now its 8-metre-high space is home to a unique kind of restaurant.

Keeping it simple extended to the kitchen which is in the middle of the restaurant and open so that the customers can see in. And they can hear too. At De Kas there was no place for a screaming chef. Yes, I know it sounds very Dutch, very reasonable, very civilised. And it was a big relief to me.

Despite, or maybe because of, the simplicity, there was a real creative buzz. We covered the walls with pictures of food from all kinds of sources, from Vogue to Donna Hay, and we dreamed up dishes that would just never occur to a Michelin-starred chef. Like roasted carrots and shin beef with salad for example.

The formula worked. De Kas is a big restaurant, seating 110 people but we were still amazed when we did 44,000 covers in our first year. It proved that people really want simply cooked food based on brilliant raw materials. After all, when you have a fantastic piece of meat or an heirloom tomato that is packed with flavour, it's just wrong to mess about with it.

In many ways De Kas was inspired by what Alice Waters has been doing for many years at Chez Panisse in California, and by Ruth Rogers and Rose Gray at the River Cafe in London. Seasonal and simple.

At first we would just do three starters: one fish, one meat, one vegetable. A typical example would be courgette flowers stuffed with mozzarella and deep-fried, served with a salsa verde made by hand using a mortar and pestle. And then there would be a barbecue dish, maybe a butterflied leg of lamb, some baked fish, something like a *tarte fine* of aubergine topped with a red pepper salsa and some cured ham.

It was all very straightforward: no foams, no reductions, no disguising. And in this way it was a huge contrast to my previous cooking experience, especially with the London kitchens from which I had just escaped.

From London to Amsterdam:
with a lot of relief

At De Kas there was no place for a screaming chef.

There was a fantastic sense of being a team. Gert Jan Hageman had business cards printed for everyone who worked there: just their name, no job description. To be part of De Kas was enough. Very Dutch, and a very good idea.

When I was there, I gave everything to De Kas. It was easy to do so, because the whole thing was just so compelling. But it took a toll, physically and mentally. After six years heading the kitchen I came close to burning out. A few weeks' rest restored me and gave me the opportunity, for the first time in ages, to think.

And the more I thought about it, the more I felt that there are cycles in your life and there comes a time to move on, no matter how proud you are of what you're doing. It also struck me that we had moved away from the totally stripped-down simplicity, rusticity even, that had been the hallmark of De Kas when we opened first. We were still keeping it simple but everything had slowly but surely become more refined, more typical of restaurant food. It was definitely time, then, to move on.

But what should I do? Stay in Holland and start again from scratch? Go back to London? And then, quite unexpectedly, a friend of mine said "I know you probably won't be interested but there's an opportunity for you...in Ireland."

Ireland? Well, yes, I knew where it was. And I knew some people who went there for the fishing. But why exchange bad Dutch weather for bad Irish weather?

I don't think I chose Ireland. In a strange kind of way it chose me. There's something a bit mystical in the way that I ended up in Ardmore knowing very little about the country beyond the climate.

Well, I had heard about Ballymaloe and I spent a while on the Wikipedia website. And I wanted a change, a real change. I think that was enough to get started in a little seaside village in West Waterford.

Order out of chaos

Learning needs to be positive and cleaning up the mess made by someone else is neither educational or positive.

It's true. There's quite a lot of yelling in restaurant kitchens. It's not just the likes of Gordon Ramsay who turn the air blue as they scream at the underlings.

The trouble is that you can end up just accepting that this is how it is in a commercial kitchen, this is the norm. But if you yell at your staff and make them frightened there are two consequences. First of all, they won't learn. You can't learn when you're scared. Remember that from school?

And the second thing is this. Staff that are abused will stay just long enough to get your name, or the name of the restaurant, onto their CVs. Which is fair enough. That's how the industry works. But it's nice when they stick around after you've invested time and energy into teaching them something.

Okay, I'll admit I didn't always think like this. There was a time when I used to yell with the rudest of them. It was my wife who pointed out that carrying on like this is counter-productive and, as usual, she was right. I was converted, literally, overnight.

Learning needs to be positive and cleaning up the mess made by someone else is neither educational or positive. At The Cliff House we clean up our own messes and it makes a good, efficient kitchen.

The other thing that helps to create the right kind of kitchen is structure. Structure is very Dutch, I know, but it gives people a sense of where they are, what they need to do. It's kind of comforting. Personally, I cope well in chaos because the first thing I do is to structure it.

Sometimes I will just stop service. We take five minutes and I say "hey, look at your section!" If the kitchen is not working properly, even in little things, it just snowballs. Much better, then, to call a halt for a few minutes and get things right back on track than having to pick up the pieces when it goes completely crazy, as it inevitably would do.

Structure is good. In fact, structure is essential. But not standardisation. There's a huge difference between standards and standardisation.

The only standardised recipe in my kitchen is for pastry and there's no doubt about it, but standardised recipes scare people. Guidelines are what you need because cooking is all about composition. You eat and taste the whole dish, not just the components. And so, what happens if you're forced to use a standardised recipe and it just doesn't taste right?

I'm not a perfectionist but I suppose I'm demanding. I like to have mouthy chefs working with me. They are not afraid to correct me, put me right. I think that's very important

and you don't get that if everyone is scared of you.

The chef, the head chef, can't do the job on his own. I know it's a cliché, but restaurants depend on teams. It's the absolute definition of team work because a restaurant kitchen demands hard work, the ability to produce good food in pretty big volumes, it demands speed and precision, all synchronised.

When you're young you sometimes think that the head chef can get away with sitting in his office all day. And some of them do, of course. But if a head chef looks busy, is really hands-on, it encourages the team. They will put in more work for you.

Stocks

These days a lot of people use stock cubes for the convenience. But in a kitchen with a reasonable sense of quality and craftsmanship you expect the real thing.

At The Cliff House we make every stock from scratch and fresh stock is just one of those things that are essential to what we do. Making stock is not magic. It's quite a logical process but there are a few key rules. Maybe the most important is to avoid simmering for too long. The reason? Every stock reaches its peak at a certain point. If you cook it beyond that point, it won't be so good.

So, the trick is to know when all of the ingredients are cooked and have released all of their flavours. This is when you need to stop the cooking process and strain. There are several things to bear in mind if you are trying to make the perfect stock:

1. Overcooking is disastrous. To take just one example, when leeks are cooked, they taste fine. Cook them for just a few more minutes and they release an off-flavour that will ruin your stock.
2. Good stock depends on clean ingredients, so always wash and peel the vegetables carefully, and rinse fish bones carefully in water. Bones and carcasses that are used to make stock should be roasted first.
3. Don't drown the flavours. Make sure that you add just enough water to cover the ingredients. You wouldn't use a litre of water with a teabag, would you?

4. You have to skim the surface of the stock regularly as it cooks. This will remove grease or dirty elements like brownish foam and small bits and pieces.
5. Only season stock when it's finished. If you use a stock in a sauce that is going to be reduced, don't season with salt.

Timing is essential for a good stock

Stocks form the base of virtually every sauce that we serve. From the filleted fish we make fish stock that is used in chowder or in sauces to go with seafood.

Stocks from beef, lamb, poultry and game bones go to make everything from a clear beef tea to a rich, dark, reduced beef jus.

However, vegetable stock is the one that we use most. Normally it's made with the peels and scrapings of vegetables that we are using in the kitchen. But this doesn't mean that the stock pot is a kind of compost bin! On the contrary, it releases the full potential of each vegetable that features in the stock. Our vegetable stock is used for lots of different things: cooking other vegetables, making sauces, jellies, foams and risottos, in the preparation of meat and fish dishes. It's amazingly versatile stuff.

Vegetable Stock (to make 1 litre)

1 fennel bulb (with the leaf)
1 medium carrot
1 medium parsnip
1 leek (only the white part)
1 white onion
¼ celeriac
¼ garlic bulb
A small bouquet of herbs wrapped in the green of the leek (3 sprigs of thyme, 1 sprig of rosemary, 5 parsley stalks, 2 bay leaves)
1 tsp of each: black peppercorns, mace, coriander seeds

- Wash and peel the vegetables and slice them all in equally sized chunks. The chunks need to be big (e.g., just cut your carrot in half) so that they don't disintegrate during the long cooking.
- Wrap the herbs in the green of the leek and hold it together with string or thread.
- Put the vegetables into a suitable pot and add the spices.
- Pour 1.5 litres of water on top of the vegetables and bring to the boil.
- Let it simmer for at least 1 hour or until the vegetables are cooked.
- Strain through a fine sieve and season to taste.

Stocks

Tip: you can freeze all stocks in the form of ice cubes and then use them as you need to.

Chicken stock

At The Cliff House, I make two kinds of chicken stock. One is made with just some water, pepper and mace and is used for glazing vegetables or oven-roasted potatoes or for a base for another sauce. The other is made with a nice assortment of vegetables to use on its own or to reduce for making sauce.

750g chicken carcasses
50g white onion
100g leek (the white part only)
100g carrot
50g celeriac
50g celery
A small bouquet of herbs wrapped in the green of the leek (3 springs of thyme, 1 sprig of rosemary, 5 parsley stalks, 2 bay leaves)
1 tsp white peppercorns, mace, fennel seeds
250ml white wine

- Preheat the oven to 200°C.
- Wash and peel the vegetables and slice them all into equally sized large chunks.
- Wrap the herbs in the green of the leek and hold it together with string or thread.
- Put the chicken carcasses on an oven tray with the vegetables.
- Roast for 15 minutes and drain the fat off the roasting tray.
- Put the chicken and vegetables in a suitable pot and add the bouquet, spices and white wine.
- Pour water on top until the ingredients are just covered and bring to a soft boil.
- Simmer for at least 3-4 hours, skimming regularly.
- Strain through a fine sieve and season to taste.

Duck stock

Duck makes a very meaty stock which can have a very intense flavour. It makes a great base for sauce.

A good long roasting will deliver a really intense stock, so much so that you can enjoy it on its own. You just strain the stock and add some seasoning and a handful of fresh chopped garden herbs.

At The Cliff House we nearly always transform duck stock into a sauce, simply by straining and then reducing until the liquid reaches the right consistency.

1 kg duck carcasses
50g white onion
100g leek (the white part only)
100g parsnip
50g fennel
2 rosemary sprigs
1 tsp each white peppercorns, star anise, coriander seeds
250ml red wine

- Preheat the oven to 200°C.
- Wash and peel the vegetables and slice them all into equally sized large chunks.
- Put the duck carcasses on an oven tray with the vegetables.
- Roast for 25 minutes and drain the fat off the roasting tray.
- Put the duck and vegetables in a suitable pot and add the herbs, spices and red wine.
- Add water until the ingredients are covered and bring to a soft boil.
- Simmer for at least 5 hours, skimming regularly.
- Strain through a fine sieve and season to taste.

Veal stock

At The Cliff House we use veal bones because they give a really intense and clean stock that can be used to make any sauce. I reduce red wine with garlic, shallots and thyme and then add the strained stock. This, in turn, is reduced to kitchen gold, so called because it is one of the most valuable substances we have to hand.

The strained bones are brought to the boil again with fresh water to make a so-called *remoulage*. This second pull provides us with the base for a new stock, and the process starts all over again. Making stock like this is self-perpetuating. In fact, it's like a living thing, the flavours intensifying all the time, going on from day to day without a break in the chain.

1 kg veal or beef bones (ask your butcher to saw them in suitable chunks for making stock)
50g shallots
100g mushrooms
50g carrots
50g leek (the white part only)
¼ garlic bulb
50g celeriac
250ml red wine
1 tsp each black pepper and juniper berries
3 sprigs of thyme
1 bay leaf

- Preheat the oven to 200°C.
- Wash and peel the vegetables and slice them all into equally sized large chunks.
- Put the bones on an oven tray with the vegetables.
- Roast for 15 minutes and drain the fat off the roasting tray.
- Put the bones and vegetables in a suitable pot and add the herbs, spices and red wine.
- Cover with water and bring to a soft boil.
- Let it simmer for at least 6 hours, skimming regularly.
- Strain through a fine sieve and season to taste.

Stocks

Lamb stock

Because we use a lot of lamb at The Cliff House, lamb stock is a perennial in the kitchen. Just as with the veal we roast the bones and reduce the end result with red wine. It goes into our lovely lamb stew for the staff and is used to glaze potatoes and vegetables that accompany lamb dishes.

1 kg lamb bones (ask your butcher to saw them in suitable chunks for making stock)
50g shallots
50g parsnip
50g carrot
50g leek (the white part only)
¼ garlic bulb
50g celeriac
250ml red wine
1 tsp black pepper
2 star anise

- Preheat the oven to 200°C.
- Wash and peel the vegetables and slice them all in equally sized large chunks.
- Put the bones on a oven tray with the vegetables.
- Roast for 20 minutes and strain the fat off the roasting tray.
- Put the bones and vegetables in a suitable pot and add the herbs, spices and red wine.

- Cover with water and bring to a soft boil.
- Let it simmer for at least 6 hours, skimming regularly.
- Strain through a fine sieve and season to taste.

Fish stock

Overcook a meat stock or a vegetable stock, and it won't taste too good. Overcook fish stock and it will taste disgusting. This is because there are oils deep in the fish bones which, if they are released, will give the stock a very nasty, chemical kind of flavour. In Dutch, we call it *tranig*. So it is critical that the balance between bones and liquid is perfectly measured and that the cooking time is kept within the 30 minute mark. Everything must be tuned to extract flavour as quickly as possible. This is why the vegetables are sliced more finely than usual, the spices are crushed and the fish bones are slightly warmed in neutral oil in order to release maximum flavour as quickly as possible.

1 kg fresh fish bones (rinsed in running water for 20 minutes)
100g leek (the white part only)
50g shallot
50g carrot
100g celery
200ml white wine

1 tsp each white peppercorns and fennel
seeds, crushed
1 bay leaf, sprig of thyme
2-3 parsley stalks
2 tbsp neutral cooking oil (such as sunflower)

- Wash and peel the vegetables.
  Slice them into 0.5 cm chunks.
- Put the oil in a suitable pot and add
  the bones and vegetables.
- Warm through on a low heat for
  3-5 minutes and then add the herbs
  and spices.
- Now add wine and bring to the boil.
- Cover with water and bring to a soft boil.
- Let it simmer for 25 minutes,
  skimming regularly.
- Strain through a fine sieve and season
  to taste.

Lobster or prawn stock

Prawn and lobster shells make unbelievably
aromatic stock. In fact, of all the things you
might think of for making stock, they are
probably the ingredients that are best suited
to the job. But you need to be very careful
as it can turn into a bitter drama if the shells
are not fresh or not cleaned properly.
And, in particular, always remember to
remove the contents of the heads.

1 kg lobster or prawn shells
80g white onion
80g leek (the white part only)
80g celeriac
80g fennel
2 plum tomatoes
1 garlic clove
200ml cider
50ml Irish whiskey
1 tsp each white peppercorns and
fennel seeds, crushed
3 basil stalks
2 tbsp neutral cooking oil (such as sunflower)

- Wash and peel the vegetables and slice
  them all into equally sized large chunks.
- Crush the shells.
- Put the oil in a suitable pot and add the
  shells and the vegetables.
- Warm through for 3-4 minutes.
- Add the whiskey and flambée, then add
  the cider, herbs and spices.
- Cover with water and bring to a soft boil.
- Simmer for 3 hours, skimming regularly.
- Strain through a fine sieve and season
  to taste.

Index a-p

Index r-z